Editing Digital Film

Integrating Final Cut Pro®, Avid®, and Media 100®

Editing Digital Film
Integrating Final Cut Pro®, Avid®, and Media 100®

Jaime Fowler

Focal Press
An imprint of Butterworth-Heinemann

Boston Oxford Auckland Johannesburg Melbourne New Dehli

Focal Press is an imprint of Butterworth–Heinemann.
Copyright © 2001 by Butterworth–Heinemann

 A member of the Reed Elsevier group

∞ Recognizing the importance of preserving what has been written, Butterworth–Heinemann prints its books on acid-free paper whenever possible.

Stills from the film *Tale of the Childcatcher* courtesy of Nunaka Valley Films.

Library of Congress Cataloging-in-Publication Data

Fowler, Jaime.
  Editing digital film : integrating Final Cut Pro, Avid, and Media 100/
  Jaime Fowler
    p.cm.
  Includes index
  ISBN: 0-24080-470-8 (pbk. : alk.paper)
    1. Motion pictures--Editing--Data processing. 2. Digital Video. I. Title.

TR899.F68 2001
778.5′35--dc21   2001023145

British Library Cataloguing-in-Publication Data
A catalogue record for this book is available from the Britis[...]

The publisher offers special discounts on bulk orders of this book.
For information, please contact:
Manager of Special Sales
Butterworth–Heinemann
225 Wildwood Avenue
Woburn, MA 01801-2041
Tel: 781-904-2500
Fax: 781-904-2620

For information on all Butterworth-Heinemann publications available, contact our World Wide Web home page at: http://www.focalpress.com

10 9 8 7 6 5 4 3 2 1

Printed in the United States of America

*For Peggy
and Lauren, Brendan,
and little Joshua*

Contents

Chapter 8: Editing Film on Media 100 NLEs with Slingshot Pro   99

Preface

The first time I heard about digital nonlinear editing was 1992. An insane visual artist named Adam walked into my video editing room to finish a trailer for his film. He explained to me that he had already cut the trailer offline and that all I had to do was make a few tweaks and assemble the rest.

During the course of our conversation, he kept bugging me about how smoothly the edit had gone. Adam is Hungarian, but the language he spoke was English. Still, I didn't understand a word of it.

"We cut all of this on an Avid. It works nonlinear. You can make a change just like that!" he exclaimed, snapping his fingers. When we set up to finish the trailer and were checking H/SC phase, Adam said, "You never have to do that in nonlinear." Every time I did a dissolve, he would say, "Oh, that's so easy with nonlinear. Just drag and drop." Every time I had to change a transition and check for H-shifts, he would say, "You don't have to do that anymore. Not with nonlinear."

He was really beginning to get on my nerves.

The advent of nonlinear editing systems has opened a lot of doors for editors, particularly with respect to mediums. Thanks to the inventors of NLE technology, video editors can become film editors, film editors can become world wide web developers, world wide web editors can become CD-ROM editors, and so on. These days, the term "editor" can apply to one who is familiar with many mediums and has adapted to many different styles of cutting.

But each medium has its niche, a set of rules that makes it different. And many times, the rules about that particular medium are cast aside, to be learned later as the project proceeds. For example, one could edit a short film for placement on the world wide web, but how do you compress it? Will the website visitors need a plug-in to see it? Which is the best compression technique for the quickest download at the highest quality? It isn't necessarily important to know these things at the outset of the project, but when the time comes to compress the film and prepare it for the world wide web, it is absolutely essential that the editor has the knowledge to properly adapt the finished cut to that medium.

In the case of filmmaking, there are many rules as well. But some of the rules of filmmaking have to be implemented from the start. If one waits until the edit is completed to learn the particulars of film, the result would prove disastrous. Unlike some mediums, film parameters have to be established from the beginning, because of the adaptation from one medium (film), to another medium (video) and then back to the original medium (film). The initial adaptation doesn't usually cause any problems. But without a proper set up from the beginning of the project, vital information can be lost, and re-adaptation from video to the original film can prove challenging, or even in some cases, impossible.

It isn't very difficult to understand how film works, but there are too many methods and means of completing film to list them in brief. Is it a DV film? Is it a 16mm film? Will it be projected in a theater? Electronically or on film? Who will conform the film? What type of numbering system will be used to identify frames of the film? Who will process the film? What about telecine? Who's the neg cutter? The list of questions could go on and on.

This book is intended for those who want to know how to adapt their nonlinear editing skills to film work. But unlike most books about film, this one is written from a video editor's perspective. I learned about film much later in my career. As a result, I don't take as much stock in one particular method of cutting film, as some film editors do. In this book, you'll learn about how to integrate film with nonlinear editing systems and some helper applications called matchbacks.

If you're an experienced editor looking for a way to cut films with nonlinear editors, or NLEs, this book is for you. If you're shooting DV but aren't sure how to put it on film, this book is for you. If you're a film editor or director without a clue as to how film and NLEs are integrated, this book is for you. And if you're a student who is learning nonlinear, but no one in your school has figured out how to use it with film, this book is definitely for you.

Learn how easy and fun it can be. Turn the page.

Jaime Fowler
March 2001

Acknowledgements

It may take a village to raise a child, but it takes a global village to write a book. Without a group of loyal associates, it's a waste of time and effort. I'll do my best to mention everyone and hope I didn't leave anyone out. Steven Hullfish, my friend, colleague, and fellow nonlinear enthusiast, has a literary touch that can be seen throughout the book. Without his kind assistance and focused perspective, I doubt that I could have finished the work in a readable manner. Alan Stewart and Mark Newman, A.C.E. have been very generous with their time, suggesting alterations and correcting some of my math. Deborah Cravey, former English professor at Clemson, helped me put this work into English, which is my native language, but not always apparently so. Nick Edgar gave me a perspective from an assistant editor's point of view, particularly with the conforming chapter. Don Nelsen taught me most of what I know about color space over a span of several years and made sure that I didn't make a fool out of myself to those who make their living studying the science of color. Patrick Krass assisted me in shooting, capturing and preparing some of the photographs and figures in this book. The folks at Film Camp™ deserve a medal for letting me run willy-nilly around the place shooting pictures and taking screenshots. Bruce Sturgill verified information to me about one of his many areas of expertise, the Media 100.

I'd also like to thank the following people for the advancement of knowledge regarding films and film systems. Their research and hard work have made a big difference in my own understanding of films, 24p, HDTV and how it is integrated with digital systems: Michael Schwartz at Sony Advanced Imaging, and Norman Hollyn for a great book about assisting (see bibliography).

Thanks to Barry Silver, Josette Hernandez, and the indefatigable Robert Mathieu at Trakker Technologies, and the good people at Focal Point Software, for their kind assistance in teaching me the details about their products.

A special thanks to my friends Janet Strauss and Angela Edwards (for using their lovely images) and David Davidson at Camera Obscura (for using his lovely script).

Thanks to the people at Focal Press for walking me through this first book with ease: Marie Lee, Lilly Roberts, Kevin Sullivan, and the rest of the Focal yokels.

I'd also like to thank my family for letting me use the kitchen table for several months in the wee hours to finish this work. One final thank you goes to whoever created the autosave function on Microsoft Word.

And now, about trademarks and their use in this book. Avid, Media Composer, Xpress, FilmScribe, AutoSync, EDL Manager, OMFI, OMF, and Avid Log Exchange are all registered trademarks of Avid Technology, Inc. Trakker, Film Trakker, Telecine Log Converter, Sound Trakker, SyncLock, and Slingshot are registered trademarks of Trakker Technologies Inc. FilmLogic is a registered trademark of Focal Point Software, Inc. Final Cut Pro, Quicktime, and Macintosh are registered trademarks of Apple Computer Inc. Film Camp is a registered trademark of Digital Media Education Center. Aaton and Aatonbase are registered trademarks of the Aaton Corporation. Cineon, Keykode, Eastman, and Kodak are registered trademarks of the Eastman Kodak Corporation. Excalibur is a trademark of Filmlab Systems. FilmLook is a registered trademark of FilmLook, Inc. CineLook is a registered trademark of Digi-Effects, Inc. Steenbeck is a registered trademark of the Steenbeck Corporation. Moviola is a registered trademark of Moviola, Inc. Cinetrim is a registered trademark of Cinetrim, Inc. Orb is a trademark of Castlewood, Inc. Zip and Jaz are trademarks of Iomega Corporation, Inc. Spirit, DataCine, Spectre and Virtual DataCine are trademark of Phillips Video, Inc. Millenium Machine is a trademark of Innovation ITK.

Chapter 1:
Tools of the Film Editor

Several years ago I was asked to consult on a "problem" film. It was a low-budget independent film (an indie) being cut in Los Angeles. The editor was very competent at cutting video, but had no idea how to cut film. The producer of the film knew that this particular editor was very competent at working with **NLEs** (non-linear editing systems), but had no idea about his editor's film experience. In other words, the editor was in over his head.

Despite what you might think about this editor's judgment, he was only doing what video editors have done for years. New video equipment is introduced all the time. For the savvy editor, it takes a short time to master new equipment. But in this case, the "new equipment" was film. Knowing the "say no once and you'll never work again" mindset of Los Angeles producers, when asked about his skill level with film, of course the editor said he could do it! In this case, the editor was trying to learn how to cut film as he went. As a result, the project was set up incorrectly from the start.

The film was cut digitally at thirty frames per second (30 **fps**), with no method of matching back to the original film frames (**matchback**) enabled on the NLE, which was an Avid. The lab, according to the producers, had not recorded key numbers and starting **time code** numbers for the beginning of each cam roll, so going back to the lab and autoconforming the film according to the time code EDL on an Excalibur was out of the question. To complicate matters even further, there was no burn-in video time code or film key numbers on the videotape transfers, and the telecine house had absolutely no database records, again, according to the producer.

So, I was asked, what's the next step?

Disaster has a uniquely slow pace. On the Titanic, people continued drinking and dancing after their ship had hit an iceberg, unaware that they were slowly sinking into the frozen waters of the North Sea. They weren't going to survive longer than a couple more hours. When it became apparent that there was trouble, all hell broke loose and everyone abandoned ship. In this case, my editor was about to abandon ship as well.

It troubles me greatly that such a foolish mistake could be made, that in haste someone would actually decide to cut a project and then try to figure out how to piece it back together. In this case, the last moments of cutting a poorly planned project seemed more like an *I Love Lucy* skit than a professional post production project.

Another example of lack of care happened more recently, again with a low-budget indie. I don't mean to pick on low-budget indies, but they are far more familiar to me. Similar mistakes have happened in my experience with filmed sit-coms and higher budget films, but it is usually the low-budget films, on which less-experienced people work, that have the biggest problems.

In this case, the film was cut. The project was complete, with a database intact and everything organized. There was only one small issue that the editor had to resolve. The key numbers displayed above picture from the NLE were not matching the key numbers on his **burn-in** video. The editor wondered, "would this be a problem?"

The answer, of course, was yes.

Somewhere along the line — we eventually pinpointed the problem to the **telecine** transfer (the process of transferring the film to videotape) — the numbers in the log had been converted from a 35mm project to 16mm gauging. As a result, the NLE was giving him frame counts up to 19, running on a base 20 scale used for 16mm instead of 16 frames per number, which is used for 35mm. Any list created by the NLE at that point would have been no good.

It's easy to become too comfortable with technology and not careful enough. In this case, the whole problem could have been avoided by looking at the tele-cine log, checking the numbers on the first clip to see that both NLE and video-tape burn-ins matched and making sure that the proper gauge of film was noted on the log. The editor claimed that he didn't have the budget to hire an assistant, who could have checked those numbers.

"Too bad," I said. "Now you're responsible."

It is for these reasons that I wrote this book. Film editing, a relatively easy subject to comprehend, is replete with small details and potential pitfalls.

Film editing has been around much longer than video. But unlike video, it has changed very little. The methods used for traditional film editing are pretty much the same as they were in the 1940s. The tools are certainly the same. In fact, many of those tools remain in use today, and they are just as accurate and useful as they ever were.

In the 1980s, equipment manufacturers were making steady attempts at uniting two very different groups of people: film editors and video editors. In those days, video editors tended to be more gadget savvy and technocratic. Film editors, on the other hand, were very hard to impress and preferred to be left to their own devices. Although a number of interim solutions were introduced in the mid and late 1980s, it wasn't until the 1990s that nonlinear editors or NLEs made an impact. The predecessors of the modern NLE were ruled out as either "too technical" or "not sophisticated enough."

In hindsight and through my own experience, I understand what made film editors standoffish when it came to new technology. Their methods were better. The thought of having to create anything in a linear manner was unthinkable.

Linear editing is like building a brick wall. It starts at the bottom and works its way up. If, when halfway through, the builder discovers that one of the bricks on the bottom is too short, he or she will have to tear down the whole wall and start over again. I can attest to this, having been through many recuts and trace edits during my tenure in television.

Film is different. The nonlinear method of cutting film is more akin to building a sand castle. It starts out by creating a basic shape that doesn't even have to look like a castle. Then, through slow trimming and sculpting of the sand, it eventually becomes a magnificent sculpture, assuming that the creator has the knack for sculpting.

Another problem for film editors was the missing element of hands-on control of the film. While they used machines to edit, film editors didn't have to trust machines to tell them which scene they were cutting or what frame they were on. They used their own eyes, hands, and good judgment for that fundamental information. As a result, the individuality of the editors seemed diminished when they were forced to use machines to tell them what they could not see: an edge number beside a frame or a grease pencil mark.

But in the early to mid 1990s, two companies began to make solid gains toward converting film and video editors toward the same type of editing equipment. Avid and Lightworks had both developed nonlinear editing machines using a means that combined the nonlinear elements of filmmaking with the technological prowess of digital video.

With the advent of NLEs, there has been a lot of crossing of traditional lines. "On line" and "Off line," terms that video editors used, became vague. Higher resolutions used with NLEs allowed creative off line editing to be completed on line. All types of editors — film, off line, and on line video— had to learn each other's trade.

But today there is still a learning gap when a video editor makes the jump to film. That gap is primarily due to a lack of understanding of how films work. In this chapter, we'll look at some of the tools and methods of traditional film editing. Later, we'll examine how they are still integrated today in even the most technical films.

A TOUR OF THE FILM CUTTING ROOM

To a modern NLE editor, the film cutting room might seem more like a museum than a work space. Nonetheless, it has served, and continues to serve, a purpose. If a director wants to see his or her film projected before the final negative is cut, the editor must come here to **conform** workprint and mag stock, the visual and aural elements used in film, using lists created by an NLE.

Nowadays these rooms are used less, but they're no less important. Conforming a workprint from an NLE cut list has to be done on an **edit bench**. It can be checked on a Moviola upright or a KEM flatbed. But the assembly of film begins here, and no matter how high tech the rest of the digital world may be, the only way to project a film is to cut film.

The survey of film editing tools begins with the traditional film cutting room. Most film cutting rooms are the same. There is always a workbench or edit bench with reel **rewinds** on either end, where the film is cut, synched, and conformed. The work bench has a synchronizer, also known as synch blocks or a **gang sync**, in between the two rewinds. Here the **workprint** and **mag stock** are synched together. There is usually a backlit portion of the table top for viewing frames. A loupe, used for looking closely at frames, is an absolute necessity. And some overhead lights are good, too. Most editors use metal long-armed clamp-on incandescent lights. These make the bench look absolutely hideous, but editors find themselves redirecting these lights all the time, so they're a must.

Figure 1.1   A typical film editing bench

And what would be the purpose of an edit bench without a splicer? Most benches have a Rivas (also called "butt") splicer on hand. Some use a guillotine splicer. Guillotine splicers are especially efficient for 16mm films. Lisa Day, the editor of many Hal Ashby films, introduced me to a **roller splicer** made in Canada. The circular blade rolls across the film when it cuts. I like this splicer, mostly because I'm left-handed and have a tendency to reach across the Rivas, which results in splicing more than just film. Splicers are equipped with rolls of splicing tape. Clear tape is used for picture, white tape for sound. The splicer is adjustable to create diagonal cuts for mag stock and straight cuts for film. Diagonal cuts are more durable and less likely to break. But a diagonal cut across a frame of film would be objectionable.

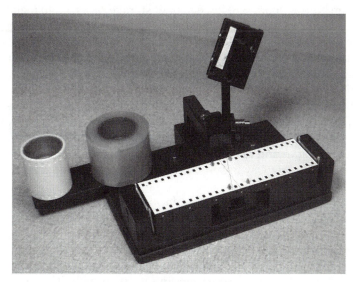

Figure 1.2   A Cinetrim roller splicer

There is always a viewing device. Different editors prefer different devices. There are two different types of devices: **uprights** and **flatbeds**. I think uprights are a lot easier to use for most purposes, but they're also very hard on workprint. As the film goes through the gate of an upright, it brushes against the bottom of the hard metal surface. I've seen a number of homemade devices that prevent the film from scratching on an upright. The most popular seems to be a velvet cloth taped to the bottom near where the film enters the gate. For smaller formats like 16mm, I prefer a flatbed, which is not only kinder and gentler on film, but also quieter than the rattle and hum of an upright.

Figure 1.3   KEM Universal Flatbed and a Moviola Upright

A typical film editing room will have a lot of storage racks, large metal bins with cloth bags used for hanging cut film clips, white boxes for storage of cam rolls, sound rolls and left-over clips that are too short to hang in a bin, film cleaner, and other knick knacks. So why am I bringing all of this up in a book about digital filmmaking? Two reasons: One, you might be asked to visit such a room. Try not to freak out. And the second reason is that you might actually be asked to work in a film editing room. If the project follows some of the workflows presented in Chapter 2, there's little reason to worry. You will only be required to conform the film to the list of numbers generated on your nonlinear editing system.

It's surprising to find how intuitive film cutting machines are. If you can align a piece of film properly in sprockets, you'll probably find the process of conforming films relatively easy.

Let's take a look at film formats and aspect ratios.

FILM GAUGES AND SHOOTING FORMATS

Motion picture uses two common gauges but many formats. The common gauges are 16mm and 35mm. 65mm is also used in extraordinary high-budget cases (65mm is the shooting equivalent of 70mm without the 5mm soundtrack area) and there is also Super Panavision 70mm.

The formats of film differ primarily in two ways: matte size, which creates the film's **aspect ratio**, and anamorphics, which is an optical solution that allows the film to be expanded for a wider aspect ratio despite its smaller original size.

A full frame of film, whether it be 16 or 35mm, has an aspect ratio very similar to video: film is 1.37:1 whereas video is 1.33:1. So why is the picture wider in the theatre? For the most part, this wasn't so before the 1950s.

The "Golden Age" of television wasn't so golden for the film world. More people were staying at home with their families in front of the tube. Box office receipts were plummeting. Many of the major studios were on the threshold of bankruptcy. Something had to be done. One of the answers to the problem was to create, promote and advertise different formats and processes. These included wider screens, brighter colors, bigger pictures and better sound.

Filmmakers found that they could create more dynamic pictures that spilled across giant screens by matting the top and bottom of the film frame and projecting it over a wider space. These mattes created a wider aspect ratio, which later became the standard for almost all theatrical releases.

One of the first of these films to come along was *The Robe*, presented in CinemaScope at a 2.35:1 aspect ratio. The wider aspect made the viewing of the film much more spectacular. As a result, box office receipts began to increase again.

Of all the mattes that were created, the 1.85:1 aspect ratio turned out to be the most popular. As a result, most films made in America still use that aspect ratio today. European films thought 1.66:1 to be a better solution, and that became their more common standard. The beauty of mattes is that there is no single standard that has to be used. Not all American films use 1.85:1. For example, Tim Burton's *Nightmare Before Christmas* was shot with a 1.66:1 matte.

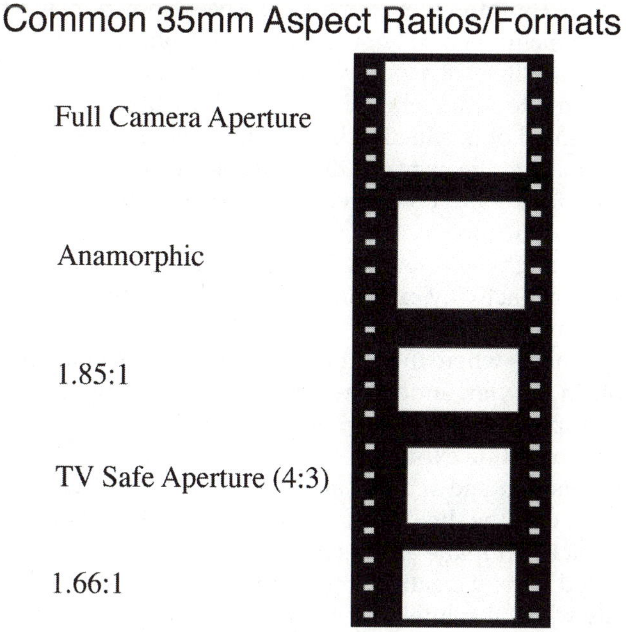

Common 35mm Aspect Ratios/Formats

Full Camera Aperture

Anamorphic

1.85:1

TV Safe Aperture (4:3)

1.66:1

Figure 1.4   Comparison of common aspect ratios/formats used in film

Anamorphics

Anamorphics is the optical science of compressing wide pictures into a more narrow frame of film and decompressing them during projection onto wide screens. Without special anamorphic camera and projection lenses, the film would look compressed when projected. The opening and closing credits of *The Sound of Music* on video is a good example of an anamorphic distortion. In order to be displayed correctly, movies must be shot and projected with the same type of anamorphic lens. In the case of some video releases where the opening and closing titles are shot in a wider scope, the aspect ratio is so large that to display it on video at the correct aspect ratio would cause the image to shrink significantly. The compromise is an elongated and somewhat distorted image.

Not all directors like anamorphics. There is a compromise in picture quality, particularly in high-contrast images, where bright light smears across the screen. Nonetheless, it is very popular with those films that use environment as part of the character of the film. Westerns with scenic panoramas and science fiction epics with fictional, futuristic worlds tend to take advantage of wider, more spectacular anamorphic aspect ratios.

Soft Mattes versus Hard Mattes

Now that the more common film formats have been shown, here's how they are created. As it was mentioned previously, an anamorphic film is created with a special type of lens. Different aspect ratios are created with mattes. There are two different types of mattes used when shooting a film, called soft and hard mattes. If the **soft matte** method of production is used, the final matte or cropping of the frame is created in negative printing, the final stage before the film is released. If a **hard matte** is used, the aspect has already been determined and the film is cropped during production.

A soft matte, might be considered a virtual matte in today's terms. That is to say, the matte doesn't actually exist on the exposed negative. Instead, the director of photography has an outline of the matte in the ground glass viewfinder of the camera. The DP knows where the matte will be, despite the fact that the entire picture is viewable in the viewfinder. The director, when using video assist, has the video monitor cropped to show where the matte will be placed and where the active portion of the frame exists.

The biggest advantage of a soft matte is that it can always be corrected. For example, if by mistake the director of photography included a stray boom microphone in the shot, a soft matte affords the opportunity to move the image higher up into the matted area by creating a new optical of the scene at the lab. Normally this is used only when absolutely necessary, as optical printing can be expensive.

Another advantage of shooting full frame and adding mattes later is that the film can be printed in full frame as well as matted, provided that proper steps were taken during the production phase. This allows an easy conversion for television at its native aspect ratio. Many DVDs provide both full aspect video and letterboxed film aspect ratios. Without a soft matte, the film must use **pan and scan** to create a full frame image within the normal television (1.33:1) aspect. This requires some hard decisions by the director as to what to include and exclude in the frame. This is becoming less necessary, as new widescreen televisions can adjust for different aspect ratios.

The advantage of a hard matte is simple: what you see is what you get (WYSIWYG). In production, post production, conforming, neg cutting, and release printing phases, the picture is always true to itself. No confusion or questions about what is on the screen. A hard matte is created during production by installing a proper matte in the matte box of the camera and exposing the **original camera negative** (OCN) with the matte in place.

Camera Rolls and Sound Rolls

Normally a film is shot on 400 foot **camera rolls**. On 16mm film, this translates to about 11 1/2 minutes. On 35mm, it's close to 4 minutes. Numbering systems for cam rolls are usually very simple. The first one is Roll 1, second is Roll 2, and so on. If two cameras are used for a scene, the numbers have letters attached. For example, cam roll 3 on the first camera is 3A, cam roll 3 on the second camera is 3B. In cases when the second camera is seldom used, the cam roll number matches the succession of single cam roll numbers. In other words, if the production is shooting a twenty-third cam roll, but it is the first cam roll using a second camera, the cam roll would be called 23B, not 1B.

Sound is recorded on location using either a time code Nagra reel to reel recorder or a time code **DAT**. Nagras appear to be getting more scarce on the set, because of the digital qualities of DAT and the ease of **SMPTE time code**. A time code DAT can go direct from the production set to an NLE. Nagra reels are seldom transferred in this fashion.

Time code DATs range in length from 30 to 90 minutes. In some higher-budget cases, the DATs are transferred to mag stock, a magnetic oxide tape that has sprockets and is the same gauge as the film. Once a cut list is completed, the editor and assistant can cut or "conform" a workprint and a mag stock copy of their digital cut on an edit bench.

In extreme cases, non-time code DAT can be used on location as well. In order to stay in the digital domain and establish frame accuracy, it must be transferred or cloned through a digital port on the machine to a time code source deck, preferably another DAT. Without this, it will not be able to redigitize the sound. Any accidental deletion of files from the NLE could prove disastrous.

NUMBERING FORMATS

Films can use several different frame numbering schemes. Each of these methods is valid, but they are used for different purposes. This section examines the most common ways used to number film frames, and how they are synchronized with sound.

Edge numbers is a frequently used and often confusing term. There are actually two different types of edge numbers: ink numbers and key numbers.

Ink Numbers

Ink numbers are printed onto workprint and mag stock after they've been synched on the editing bench. Ink numbers are used a lot less on NLE projects these days because material can be synched in the NLE after it is transferred on a telecine instead of on an edit bench. However, if the budget allows conforming a workprint during an edit on an NLE, ink numbers could be used as a reference. There are lots of different ways to cut films, which are examined in Chapter 2.

Ink numbers are divided into three components: a prefix, which is two alphanumeric characters for 16mm and three for 35mm; the leading numbers, which come in two varieties as well, four digit and five digit; and a frame count, which is not a visual part of the ink number, but is used to identify frames between ink numbers. Usually the prefix numbers match each synched roll of film. Most major studios have individual methods of numbering ink numbers on their films. Alphabetic characters can be used, so that synch roll letters are not confused with cam roll numbers. The original intent of the prefix was for shot numbers, which is the English method of shooting films. Instead of using scene numbers as a guide, each shot is numbered and the ink numbers reflect that number in the prefix. So shot 1 would have a prefix of 01, and so forth. Ink numbers are more difficult to track, so a code book is needed. The code book shows the relationships between ink numbers and the latent edge numbers on the OCN and workprint. It also shows the relationships for original recorded sound and the mag stock that is used to conform the workprint.

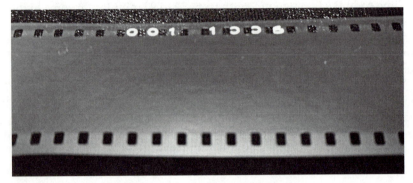

Figure 1.5   Ink Numbers on workprint
This 35mm mag stock has a three digit prefix followed by four leading numbers.

Key Numbers

Key numbers, also called latent edge numbers, are more commonly used with NLEs. Key numbers are generated along the edge of the film after it is processed. They are a physical part of the film and don't require inkjet printing, as ink numbers do. When a workprint is made, the key numbers match the ones on the OCN, or original camera negative. Using this method, it is a lot easier to conform the OCN after the cutting is done. Beside the key number on the film's edge is a bar code, known as the **Key code**. This bar code can be read by most telecine machines and makes it easy for the **colorist** to database frame numbers to use in an NLE. 35mm films have a new key number every 16 frames for each foot of film. Kodak 16mm films change key numbers every 20 frames, or 6 inches of film. Some other 16mm film manufacturers have key numbers every 12 inches or 40 frames. To accurately keep track of each frame beyond the key number, a frame count is added.

One of the problems with the use of key numbers is that they are indeed latent. In other words, if there is a light leak in the camera and the film edge is exposed, it could actually overexpose the key number, so that the telecine (or anyone or anything else) could not read it. Still, it is much more advantageous in the realm of NLEs to use key numbers than to revert to a code book.

The key numbers identify certain traits of the film, including the manufacturer, the stock type, a prefix identifying the roll and a footage count. For example, the key number KN 91 1246 7990 indicates that the film used is Eastman 7292 stock (see Table 1.1). Every manufacturer uses a different prefix for each stock.

The key code reveals the same information as the human-readable key numbers, but adds information about the date of manufacture of the film.

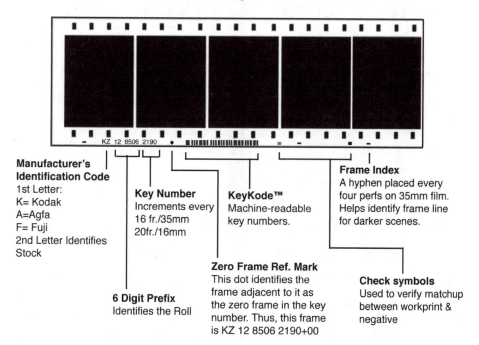

Film Markings- Identifying Features of 35mm Film

Manufacturer's Identification Code
1st Letter:
K= Kodak
A=Agfa
F= Fuji
2nd Letter Identifies Stock

Key Number
Increments every
16 fr./35mm
20fr./16mm

KeyKode™
Machine-readable
key numbers.

Frame Index
A hyphen placed every four perfs on 35mm film. Helps identify frame line for darker scenes.

6 Digit Prefix
Identifies the Roll

Zero Frame Ref. Mark
This dot identifies the frame adjacent to it as the zero frame in the key number. Thus, this frame is KZ 12 8506 2190+00

Check symbols
Used to verify matchup between workprint & negative

Figure 1.6   Identifying Marks on 35mm Film

Time Code

Time code is used as a method for counting frames with videotape. From its beginning in the mid 1960s time code was never accurate. Time code measured the frame rate of video at 30 fps, when in fact the frame rate is 29.97 fps. For years, this was not a problem. In the late 1970s, a combination of automated equipment and syndicated television significantly changed that. Broadcast playback was measured by a clock in real time. But a program that ran 28:30 minutes using 30 fps time code was actually a couple of seconds longer. So the automated equipment ended the program abruptly and went to a commercial. Unfortunately, the last two seconds of the program was usually the syndicator's logo.

Table 1.1 Key code Number IDs

ID	Maker	Stock	ID	Maker	Stock
KA	Kodak	5243/7243	KU	Kodak	5279/7279 Vision 500T
KB	Kodak	5247/7247	KV	Kodak	5244/7244
KC	Kodak	5297/7297	KW	Kodak	5287/7287
KD	Kodak	5234/7234	KX	Kodak	SFX 200T
KE	Kodak	5222/7222	KY	Kodak	5620/7620 PT 640T
KF	Kodak	5295	KZ	Kodak	5274/7274 Vision 200T
KG	Kodak	5294/7294	EA	Kodak	5285
KH	Kodak	5231/7231	FI	Fuji	FCI (01)
KI	Kodak	5246/7246 Vision 250D	FN	Fuji	F-64 (10)
KJ	Kodak	5296/7296	FN	Fuji	FCI (13)
KK	Kodak	5245/7245	FN	Fuji	F-500 (14)
KL	Kodak	5293/7293	FN	Fuji	F-64D (20)
KM	Kodak	5248/7248	FN	Fuji	F-125 (30)
KN	Kodak	7292	FN	Fuji	F-250 (50)
KO	Kodak	5249/7249	FN	Fuji	F-250D (60)
KP	Kodak	5600 PT	FN	Fuji	F-500 (70)
KQ	Kodak	5277/7277 Vision 320T	AN	Agfa	XT 100
KR	Kodak	5289/7289 Vision 800T	AM	Agfa	XTR 250

Table 1.1   Key code Number IDs (continued)

ID	Maker	Stock	ID	Maker	Stock
KS	Kodak	5272/7272	AF	Agfa	XT 320
KT	Kodak	5298/7298	AS	Agfa	XTS 400

Note that Fuji Keykode ID "FN" refers to several different stocks. To decode the exact stock used, it is necessary to read the barcode, which has a numbering system instead of lettering. The bar code ID number is in parentheses.

The result was the use of a new, more accurate form of time code. To distinguish between the two, the accurate version was called **drop frame** because it "dropped" two numbers of frames every minute except for every tenth minute, which maintained accurate timing according to the 29.97 fps play rate. The traditional 30 fps measuring method was called **nondrop frame**.

It is important to note that drop frame never truly drops a frame. It drops the names of the frames. The number of frames is the same in nondrop frame time code and drop frame time code, but the names of the frames differ between the two. This could be compared to high-rise buildings that have at least thirteen floors. They always have a 13th floor, but they often skip the floor number 13, going from 12 to 14.

Both of these types of measurement are still used today. Broadcasters generally prefer drop frame, although it should be noted that some still stick to the old way. Many of the programs that I edited for PBS used nondrop frame. As a result, a standard 30 minute show, with a running time of 28:38 was actually came in at 28:36:08 using nondrop time code.

Animators, advertisers, and filmmakers tend to avoid drop frame time code. Animators find the loss or dropping of frames confusing. When each frame of animation is created, a dropped frame can confuse the count of actual frames produced. For the filmmaker, it can cause a numeric inconsistency for gauging pulldown. If a telecine transfer is made and it is assumed that every fifth frame of time code is a telecine A frame, for example, what happens at the top of every minute when that count is altered by two frames? The consistency goes away. As a result, filmmakers usually insist that nondrop frame time code be used both for picture and sound.

Advertisers tend to use nondrop frame for another reason. Their end product, normally under a minute, doesn't require any end-of-minute adjustments to maintain consistency. A 30-second spot will not need a frame adjustment.

With filmmaking, the rule is simple: use nondrop frame time code.

Production Notes

There is no doubt that a film generates more paperwork than any television or video product ever could. Perhaps the best reason for this is that there are so many people working on so much footage that the more information given, the better the odds of successfully working with the materials. As a result, **logs** of information are kept so that film editors can understand what took place during the production.

A typical production uses these logs and reports:

Script supervisor daily production report or log
Facing pages
Lined script
Camera reports
Sound reports

Script Supervisor Daily Log

Some new directors of low-budget films make the poor decision not to hire a **script supervisor**. This almost always results in catastrophe. A good script supervisor can make the post production process smooth through the use of informational tools such as the script supervisor daily log. This log is full of details that can prevent the editor from wasting time looking for missing footage.

On every shooting day, the script supervisor prepares a log. The log is a journal of sorts, with complete details on which scenes were shot on which cam rolls and sound rolls and which takes the director wants to print. A typical log will contain

Production title
Director
Date
Production company
Script supervisor

It also contains entries for each shot, including

Cam roll number
Sound roll number
Slate (scene number)
Print (selected take numbers, chosen by the director)
Time (duration of the shot in minutes:seconds)
Description

The description usually contains a few words about the subject and framing of a shot. It may also contain information that the director requests be put into the log.

Facing Pages

Facing pages are given their name because they are printed on the back of a sheet of three ring paper instead of on the front. Their purpose is to be placed opposite a corresponding script page, so that the editor may look at all of the information about a scene with the script on the other side of the open binder.

Each facing page has an entry for the corresponding script page that it should face. They are one-sided, so that additional pages may be added when necessary. For some films, the facing pages have such copious notes that they do not all face the correct page. In these cases, the pages are placed together so that the editor can find the one that corresponds with the scene they are cutting.

Facing pages have much of the same information as a daily log, with more explicit descriptions, remarks, and lens length. The remarks usually have some information about the director's preference, or note any mistakes were on any of the takes. They also contain information about changes in the blocking or in the script and how they were dealt with on the set.

Facing pages also have **circled takes**, which help the editor determine the director's preferred take. Facing pages may not always explain why certain takes were preferred over others, but that is usually evident in the **dailies** themselves.

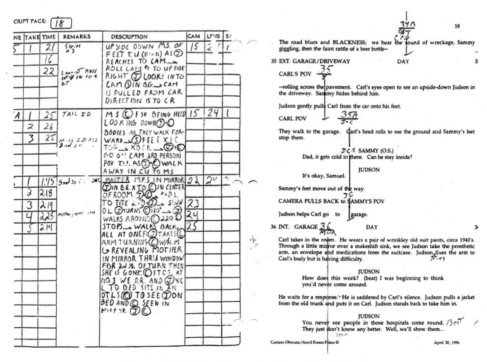

Figure 1.7   Facing Pages next to a Lined Script.

Lined Scripts

Lined scripts provide the editor with a visual representation of what is happening on camera over the course of the script. Script supervisors create lined scripts to let the editor know circled takes and coverage for the scene. A typical lined script would contain

> Scene number
> Circled takes
> A straight line during dialog to indicate that the persons speaking are covered in the shot
> A squiggly line during dialog to indicate that the persons speaking are not in the shot
> A brief shot description, such as MS- Dan Keitz in living room
> In some cases, an audio or video time code for the start of the shot

When used with facing pages, the lined script contains all of the items necessary to edit a scene. These tell the story of what was intended and what actually happened. Other elements, such as sound and camera reports can also be used as a reference.

Camera Reports

Camera reports are created by the camera department and contain information about what was shot on each camroll, including

> Cam roll Number
> Scene/take
> Length of shot (in footage)
> Total footage per roll
> Frame rate (normally 24)
> Date
> Notes
> Camera operator or assist name
> Circled takes (chosen by the director)

Circled takes can be noted in NLEs by either adding a Print column to an electronic bin or using an asterisk (*) next to a **clip name**. Any uncircled takes are also referred to as **B-Neg** and aren't always telecined or printed, depending on the budget.

Sound Reports

Sound reports are the sound department's equivalent of a camera report. The sound reports have more precise information, because SMPTE time code can be noted during recording of sound. A sound report will contain

Sound roll number
Scene/take
SMPTE time code
Date
Sound mixer name
Notes
Circled takes

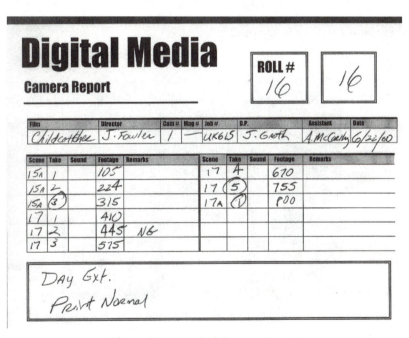

Figure 1.8   A typical Camera Report

Code Books

Code books are post production logs for recording the relationship of scenes with ink numbers, key numbers, sound rolls, cam rolls, lab rolls, and time code. Primarily used for tracking ink numbers to their original cam roll and corresponding key numbers, a code book is a regular item in most film cutting rooms.

Code books aren't always necessary in a digital editing suite. The database of materials is already recorded in an electronic bin, the result of an automated telecine log, which records the numbers automatically. But a code book is a very handy reference in either room, particularly if there is doubt regarding the validity of the database, or if ink numbers are used.

Slates

A slate is the best visual representation of what happened on each shot in the dailies. The slate should contain both audio and visual information. In some cases, if the shot is without sound (**MOS**), the sound person will do the audio slate anyway. The slate should contain the production name, director, director of photography (DP), scene and take and shoot date.

There is also a "smart slate" that will generate audio time code information in an LED array located at the top of the slate. This makes it much easier to sync sound with picture. An editor can check the smart slate against the database in the NLE to ensure that the audio time code matches. In some situations, audio time code will have to be entered manually. Audio time code should always be recorded using nondrop frame mode.

Figure 1.9   Smart Slate

When Good Notes Go Bad

If the camera reports don't match sound reports on circled takes or the facing pages don't have information that agrees with the rest of the production notes, it is best to call the script supervisor. This person is in charge of keeping track of the various reports and should have accurate answers. Any of the production paperwork that doesn't jibe is the responsibility of the script supervisor. Going over the supervisor's head to the director is considered bad form and can create more problems.

It's important to get to the bottom of these minor problems before they become big problems downstream. As the late Alabama football coach Paul "Bear" Bryant once said, "It's the little things that'll git ya."

Now that the tools of filmmakers have been examined, let's move on to some of the workflows for post production.

Chapter 2:
Post Production
Workflow

There is an old saying that if you don't know where you're headed, you'll never get there. This certainly rings true when it comes to the creation of a motion picture. It is fascinating to see how each filmmaker works, because there are so many different ways to create film. And no two filmmakers work exactly alike.

The first step to successfully creating a film is to define a path or plan, a workflow of how the film will be produced from beginning to end. Some of these workflows are elaborate, resembling architectural drawings for skyscrapers. Others are written on the back of a piece of cardboard. It doesn't really matter. But without a workflow, every phase of production will suffer. Some filmmakers lack the experience to create a workflow, as parodied in the films *American Movie* and *Bowfinger*. The workflow is the key to finishing any film successfully, whether it be a low-budget slasher or a blockbuster extravaganza.

The post production workflow is normally determined by above-the-line staff, usually the line producer. The line producer develops this workflow with the director in preproduction meetings. It is the responsibility of the editor to notify the producer of any proposed changes in the workflow that could affect the process. The line producer must always be made aware of how the process will change, particularly with respect to how money is being spent on services and supplies. Any alteration in the work flow could potentially cause a waste of resources, loss of available personnel, or a loss of monies reserved for services in the budget. Post production services, such as telecine, lab work, and editing facilities, are prearranged by the production company. If the editor determines that a change is necessary, he or she must first consult with the line producer for approval. Failure to do so could result in dismissal.

One of the biggest flaws in writing about film post production workflow is that no matter how adamant one is about the "proper" methods used for film creation, there is at least another who will say, "we don't do it that way." And there is far more variance in the process of filmmaking than of videomaking.

Why? One reason is that filmmaking, particularly film editing, can use a wider variety of methods and tools than video can. Some filmmakers developed their methods of post production long ago. For others, their post methodology develops as rapidly as technology itself. Many theatrical motion pictures are edited concurrently with the production phase, a method rarely used in video editing. By bringing in the post production team at an early stage, the director can find continuity, scripting, action, and editing flaws early in production and seek solutions while the film is still being shot on location. Of course, this isn't always possible. Some films don't begin post production until after principal photography is completed. Any reshoots or pickup shots are done after the first edit, when flaws and needs of the film are detected.

Low-budget films, particularly those with little planning, can unwisely eliminate production crew positions that seem too expensive, such as a script supervisor or continuity person. These seemingly economic decisions can lead to disastrous consequences in post. The end result is that the fledgling director learns a lesson and the editor is made to suffer the result of a bad decision. It has happened many times. As long as there are new and inexperienced directors, this problem will no doubt continue.

This chapter examines some post production workflows, from high-budget feature films to ultra-low-budget indies. It also explores a workflow for the relatively new method of digital video (DV) filmmaking. In the process of doing so, one can get a pretty good idea of the different approaches to post production of a motion picture.

THREE WORKFLOW SCENARIOS

Here are some different scenarios for post production. Keep in mind that none of these are necessarily the exact way that any film is edited. There is more than one way to skin a cat.

The High-Budget Film Workflow

As mentioned previously, it is desirable in most higher budget films for the editing staff to commence work immediately once the principal photography phase begins. If shooting takes place on a soundstage, it is common for the editing crew to be placed in a nearby building, so that the director can walk a short distance to look at dailies. As production continues, the editors and assistants are deluged with questions from the set. Will this work, or, what are we going to do about that? How will we be able to cut from this scene to the next? All of the questions can be answered a short distance away.

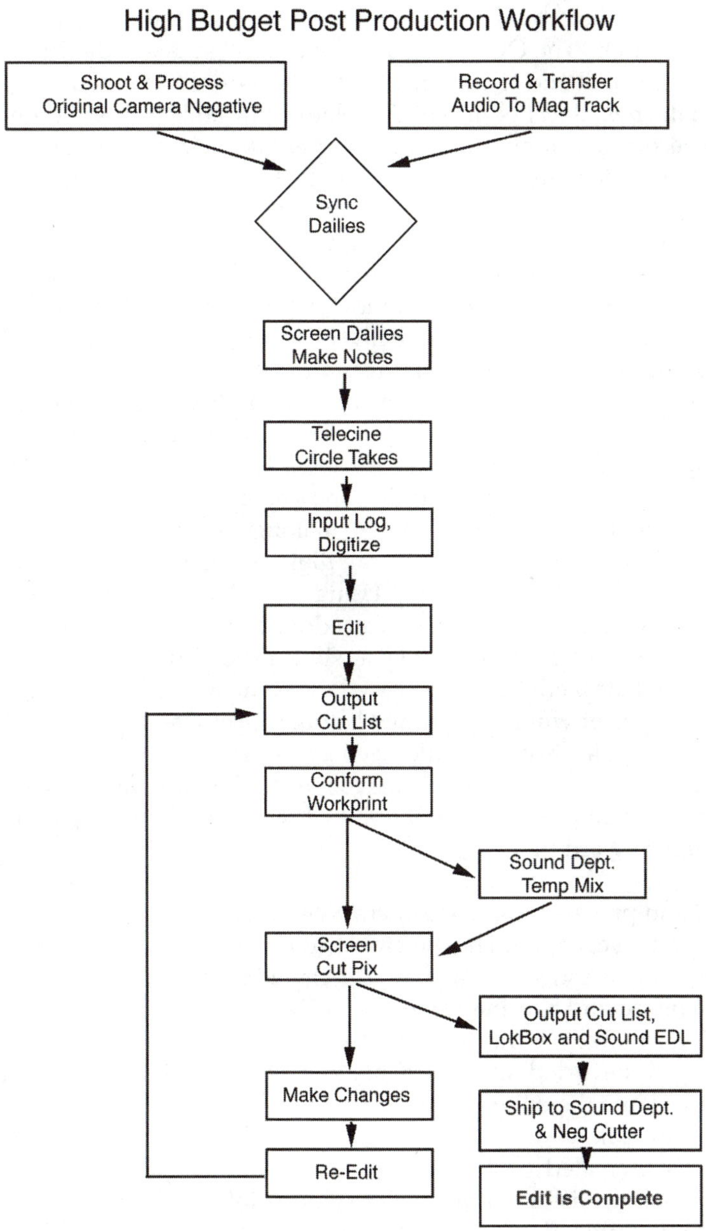

High Budget Post Production Workflow

```
┌──────────────────────┐        ┌──────────────────────┐
│   Shoot & Process     │        │   Record & Transfer   │
│ Original Camera Negative│      │  Audio To Mag Track   │
└──────────────────────┘        └──────────────────────┘
              ╲                    ╱
               ◇ Sync
                 Dailies
                    │
           ┌──────────────────┐
           │  Screen Dailies   │
           │    Make Notes     │
           └──────────────────┘
                    │
           ┌──────────────────┐
           │     Telecine      │
           │   Circle Takes    │
           └──────────────────┘
                    │
           ┌──────────────────┐
           │    Input Log,     │
           │     Digitize      │
           └──────────────────┘
                    │
           ┌──────────────────┐
           │       Edit        │
           └──────────────────┘
                    │
           ┌──────────────────┐
           │      Output       │
           │     Cut List      │
           └──────────────────┘
                    │
           ┌──────────────────┐
           │     Conform       │
           │    Workprint      │
           └──────────────────┘
                    │        ╲
                    │     ┌──────────────────┐
                    │     │   Sound Dept.     │
                    │     │    Temp Mix       │
                    │     └──────────────────┘
           ┌──────────────────┐
           │      Screen       │
           │     Cut Pix       │
           └──────────────────┘
                    │        ╲
                    │     ┌──────────────────┐
                    │     │  Output Cut List, │
                    │     │LokBox and Sound EDL│
                    │     └──────────────────┘
                    │                │
           ┌──────────────────┐  ┌──────────────────┐
           │   Make Changes    │  │ Ship to Sound Dept.│
           └──────────────────┘  │   & Neg Cutter    │
                    │            └──────────────────┘
           ┌──────────────────┐          │
           │     Re-Edit       │  ┌──────────────────┐
           └──────────────────┘  │  Edit is Complete │
                                 └──────────────────┘
```

Figure 2.1   A High-Budget Post Production Workflow

When a film is shooting on location, it was previously more common for the editing crew to stay at the production company's home city and discuss these problems by phone or fax. The OCN would be shot, selected takes (dailies) would be workprinted, synched and transferred, and the editorial crew would begin working on them the next day. Because of the relative portability of NLEs, on-location editing has become far more common. *Homeward Bound II* was shot in Vancouver, B.C., at the old Molson Brewery. There was plenty of room in the administration building for nonlinear equipment, so the Avids were set up there. Looking at dailies or checking a continuity problem meant a short stroll across the brewery.

In some cases, where locations were a bit more remote, NLEs have been installed in mobile facilities. On the motion picture *Assassins*, Sony Pictures Digital Editorial (SPDE) set up a recreational vehicle with two NLEs inside. SPDE manager Stephen Cohen oversaw the creation of this vehicle and it worked quite well for the editorial crew, who could move from location to location with relative ease. Director Richard Donner and editor Richard Marks could view dailies, discuss continuity issues, and play back completed scenes in a comfortable environment, even while situated in the middle of nowhere.

Advancements in this technology are making it even easier and better for editors at remote locations. Most NLEs can **digitize** "on the fly," that is, record immediately with a click of the mouse. Using the video tap from a film camera, which is normally used for video assist, an editor could conceivably sit in a trailer and record the takes on location as they are being shot. The big advantage would be almost immediate feedback on how well the scene would cut. If there were any problems, the director would be notified before the set was struck. The drawback would be that anything edited would need proper entry of edge numbers in the database at a later time, a lamentable task for even the most valiant assistant.

With those examples in mind, the workflow of a big-budget picture follows a fairly straightforward path.

1. Shoot and process Original Camera Negative.
2. Workprint everything. The director is going to want to see projected dailies.
3. Using camera and sound reports, the circled takes selected by the director are synched and telecined from the OCN to videotape. During telecine, a log is created of the transferred takes.
4. The log is converted into a readable format by the NLE and the footage is digitized into the editing system.
5. The editor edits.
6. A cut list is created.
7. The cuts in the list are conformed to workprint.
8. The cut is screened.

So far, so good, right? Here's where everyone on the edit crew can take a breather. A little calm before the storm.

9. Changes are made.
10. The editor re-edits the film.
11. The new cut list or a change list is made.
12. Workprint is reordered if necessary and conformed.
13. The film is screened…again.

And so it goes. Steps 9-13 are repeated until a solid cut of the film is achieved. After that, it goes to the sound department. The picture cut is complete.

There are quite a few variances that can occur in this workflow. One is that the director may not need to have workprint of all of the dailies on hand before cutting begins. But it's much better to view all of the footage on the big screen. Dailies can be screened with the director and notes can be made early in the process. In such a case, the dailies would need to be synched and coded, then transferred. This method was used on *Homeward Bound II*. The editors wanted to see the dailies on a flatbed, sometimes with the director on hand. So the assistants took the workprint, synched it with mag stock, coded it, and left the synch rolls on the flatbed until late afternoon for any necessary viewing. After that, the lead assistant would take the workprint to telecine, transfer it, and digitize it into the NLE. The next morning, the editors would cut those scenes.

In other cases, the assistants might conform workprint concurrently as it is being cut on the NLE. For example, the editor might have a good draft of Scene 26. The director wants to see it, so the assistants conform it from workprint and mag stock. The scene is screened on an interlock projector and change notes are made.

This method has served many features well, however this is a capital intensive workflow, and budget constraints may prevent some productions from working in this manner. The next examples will address a workflow with tighter purse strings.

The Medium-Budget Film Workflow

These days, a "medium-budget film" is ill defined. In Hollywood, a $6 million dollar film would be considered low budget. But the recent rise of ultra-low-budget filmmaking lowers the bar a bit. So for these purposes, a medium-budget film is one that can't quite afford the luxuries of high-budget techniques. In this case, the methods define it a lot better than the budget.

Medium-budget films are deceiving, in that they may use some of the techniques of higher-budget films and yet cut costs in other more extraordinary ways. For example, I used *Homeward Bound II*, a medium-budget film, in the previous examples of high-budget films. It did have some workflow methods that high-budget films use, but in most ways it was a medium-budget film. One of the cost cutting methods on *HBII* was the use of non-time code DAT machines for recording the character voices of the dogs and cats in the film. DAT machines, particularly those that utilize SMPTE time code, can be fairly costly. To cut costs, Disney used a high-end prosumer DAT machine and recorded SMPTE time code on

Medium Budget Post Production Workflow

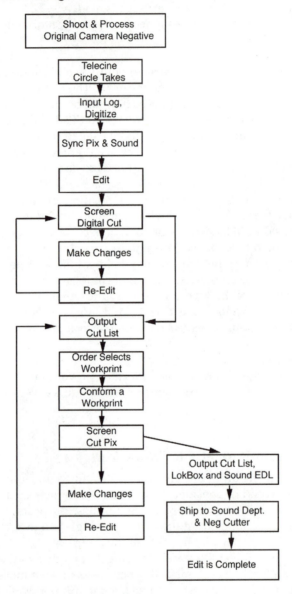

Figure 2.2 A Medium-Budget Post Production Workflow

audio track 2. This saved them several thousand dollars, and took very little extra work on the NLE (an Avid), which could read audio time code.

The mark of most medium-budget films is a reduced use of traditional film editing and increased dependency on NLEs as synching and screening devices. Like their high-budget cousins, medium-budget films still rely on screening of a workprint, but only in the final stages of post production.

Because of the ability to synchronize sound and picture inside an NLE, medium-budget films can use the latent edge numbers of a film and the SMPTE time code from DAT machines as a method of synching and later conforming the film. This eliminates the need for creating ink code on workprint and mag stock.

All of the synching can be done inside the NLE as opposed to telecine, where it is much more expensive.

Here then, is an example of a medium-budget post production workflow.

1. Shoot original camera negative.
2. Using camera reports, the circled takes are telecined MOS from the OCN to videotape. During telecine, a log is created of the transferred takes.
3. The log is converted into a readable format by the NLE and the footage is digitized into the editing system. Sound is digitized into the NLE using sound reports, going direct from the original time code DAT.
4. Both sound and picture are synched in the NLE by an assistant.
5. The editor edits.
6. A digital cut is screened on the NLE.
7. Changes are made, usually in the form of a list, sometimes one by one with the director on hand.
8. The editor re-edits the film.

From this point, steps 5-8 are repeated until a truly "screenable cut" is completed. Once the director green-lights the cut, a workprint is ordered of the scenes in the NLE cut and the workprint is conformed using the cut list from the NLE.

9. A cut list is created.
10. The editor outputs sound directly from the NLE. Sound is transferred to mag stock for screening on an interlock projector with the workprint.
11. The cuts in the list are printed from the OCN to workprint.
12. The workprint is conformed.
13. The film is screened, with sound and picture interlocked.

Usually, steps 9-13 are repeated at least twice more before the project goes to the sound department.

These methods, though somewhat constrained by budget, allow for enough flexibility for the editor and director to work together in a fairly comfortable arrangement with some margin for error. The next workflow deals with less comfortable conditions, particularly with respect to monies and resources.

The Ultra-Low-Budget Film Workflow

When I first started working in Dallas as a television editor, I learned a valuable lesson. A client had given me a fairly sizable project, ridden with problems. It was a musical, with theatrical lighting and a lot of shaky handheld camera work. The cameras would start and stop intermittently, making match cuts impossible. Matching color seemed out of the question. With a large ensemble cast, the camera never seemed to be on the right actor at the right time. And the music? Yikes! The sound crew must have fallen asleep at the console.

The producer, a kindly good ole boy type, asked me "What do you think?" I managed to sputter out a laundry list of serious issues, much like the ones mentioned above. "We already know *what's wrong with it*," he replied. "I meant, *what can you do for it?*" In a single moment, I came to realize that the director has seen the production many more times than I, and that their purpose in working with an editor is to gain insight into the solutions, not the problems of their production. Stephen Hullfish, the supervising editor at DHV TV in Chicago, put it best: "An editor is a solver of problems, not the creator."

Every film has problems. Listen to the director's track on any DVD. Talk to the editors of big-budget films. Money may add production value, but it doesn't necessarily prevent problems.

In *Saving Private Ryan*, the eight American soldiers looking for Ryan enter a village. One is killed by a sniper's bullet. In a later scene, it cuts to a wide shot of the men combing the terrain of a large green field, and there are eight of them again. *Titanic* shows the entryway to the first class dining room, a glass door. And in the door, the reflection of the camera crew is seen. *Planes, Trains and Automobiles* had to reshoot an entire crowd scene in the train station, because a crowd of onlookers (not extras) had gathered to see Steve Martin and John Candy. The problem was that the windows of the train showed the reflection of the onlookers.

So every film has issues, including high-budget films. But big-budget films have the money to solve them. Low-budget pictures can't afford this luxury.

The late Edward Dmytryk, considered by many the father of **film noir** and an excellent editor himself, once defined three types of editors: the mechanic, the cutter and the miracle worker.

A mechanic is a button-pushing automaton, who offers little more to a film than the ability to operate equipment, follow the script verbatim and do exactly as the director says. The cutter is a creative person who sees the film as the audience sees it and can offer solutions, alternative viewpoints, and new ideas on how to finish the film. But the miracle worker can get the director out of any fix, repair any problem, come up with a better solution to any issue.

Every ultra-low-budget film needs a miracle worker. When reshoots are impossible, ADR (automatic dialog recording) improbable, and compromises are inevitable, it is the task of the film editor to make a low-budget picture watchable. Not everyone can do this. Not everyone *wants* to do it.

Ultra Low Budget Post Production Workflow

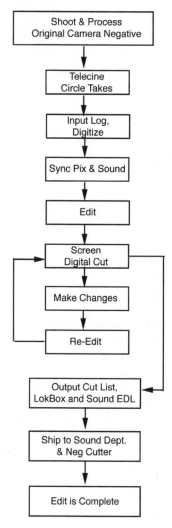

Figure 2.3   An Ultra-Low-Budget Post Production Workflow

There are more variables than ever in a low-budget post production scenario. Creative budgeting calls for some daring techniques. Here's one example:

1. Shoot original camera negative.
2. Using camera reports, the circled takes are telecined MOS from the OCN to videotape. During telecine, a log is created of the transferred takes.
3. The log is converted into a readable format by the NLE and the footage is digitized into the editing system. Sound is digitized into the NLE using sound reports.
4. Both sound and picture are synched in the NLE by an assistant.
5. The editor edits.
6. A digital cut is screened on the NLE.
7. Changes are made, usually in the form of a list, sometimes one by one with the director on hand.
8. The editor re-edits the film.
9. Repeat steps 5-8 until the film is completed.

In this scenario, every screening takes place on an NLE. Most directors would like to see their work projected before it goes to the neg cutter. In most ultra-low-budget films, they never will be projected on a big screen. Instead, they go straight to tape, so there's no reason to even attempt to screen them outside of the NLE environment.

But it's very risky to go from NLE to neg cut. If there are any mistakes made, a cut neg cannot be replaced. In these situations, it's a good idea to send a digital cut on videotape to the neg cutter along with your cut list and sound EDLs.

I haven't mentioned a lot about sound, but in the case of ultra-low-budget films, it's very important. In higher-budget films, an EDL of the sound cuts is made. That way, the sound department can conform the time code numbers in the list from the original DATs directly onto their digital audio workstations. In lower-budget films, the sound is often taken directly from the NLE onto a DAT, which saves conforming time. This makes the picture cutter a sound cutter as well. On an ultra-low budget, the sound effects, mixing and music might all be done on the NLE. Most picture editors don't particularly like doing this, but it happens—a lot.

If the film goes directly from NLE to an **answer print**, there might be a few surprises. Some of the low-budget wonders that we've completed through the Film Camp program have used this method. The best solution is to project the NLE cut on a large format television. At Film Camp, we use a 60-inch projection TV. Subtle reactions become easy to read. Marginal production errors are amplified. Even small plot twists can seem contrived. A large screen will amplify every intention of the filmmaker. So if any money is available in the budget, a filmmaker should at least consider projecting on a large format screen. Making a workprint of the NLE edit for a theater screen is even better.

DV FILM WORKFLOW

Digital video, better known as DV, is deceiving. Although it may seem to be a much less expensive method of filmmaking, getting the video back to film can be an expensive, unforgiving, and time consuming process.

Some of the latest versions of NLEs offer uncompressed video output. I highly recommend that this type of system is used as the final video source. There are others that tout "full resolution DV," but these systems use a codec, a compressor-decompressor, and the resolution is compromised. In fact, when any effect is placed on a DV source in an NLE, it leaves the digital domain.

In the ever-changing world of video technology, one thing is sure: the resolution, format, contrast ratio, and colorimetry of video pictures will improve. The near future offers high-definition formats, progressive scan frames, and wider screens. Soon it will be hard to tell the difference between video- and film-originated pictures. But for now, it's pretty easy. So choose your format wisely.

Here's an example of a DV project workflow

1. Principal photography (shooting on video).
2. Transfer the DV tape onto another format for cutting. DV videotape is a very thin 8mm metal tape. It's better to work from a more durable and stable source instead of the original. When the final high-resolution redigitizing is done, use the originals.
3. Using a log or script supervisor notes, digitize the selected takes from DV to NLE.
4. The editor edits.
5. A digital cut is screened on the NLE.
6. Changes are made, usually in the form of a list, sometimes one by one with the director on hand.
7. The editor re-edits the film.

Steps 5-7 are repeated until the film is completed.

8. Rebatch digitize the entire film at the highest resolution of your NLE. It's best to use an uncompressed resolution with color correction.
9. Send the videotape to the video-to-film transfer facility.
10. Screen the film and make changes when necessary and/or possible.

Like the low-budget scenario, a DV film will be screened on the NLE. I highly recommend the use of a large format projection television or monitor. It's easier to detect some of the subtleties and errors previously mentioned.

The final stages of DV filmmaking are the most critical. Choosing a method of transfer and solving the problems associated with DV can be difficult. For more information on the processes involved, see Chapter 10.

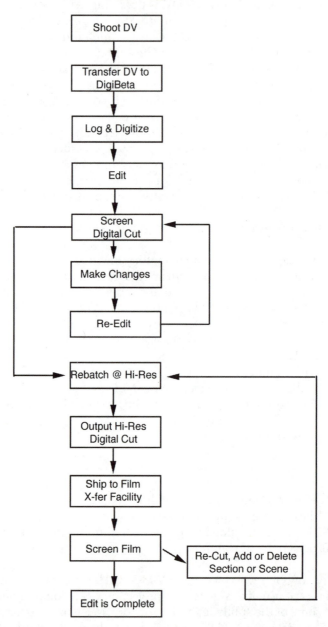

Figure 2.4   A DV-To-Film Workflow

Chapter 3:
Telecine Demystified

Do you like math? If you do, you're going to love telecine. Telecine is the process of transferring film to video. The telecine process necessitates a bit of math, because neither NTSC nor PAL video have the same number of frames per second as film, and NTSC requires a 3:2 pulldown in order to equate 24 fps to 30 fps. But NTSC video actually runs at 29.97 fps, so the telecine has to slow down to 23.97 fps. This means that the sound will have to be slowed down .01 percent, which makes the math even more fun!

When film is transferred through a telecine, it is normally running at about 24 frames per second, which is its standard projection speed. Telecines don't use light to scan the frames of film. Instead, they scan the picture with a gas beam. The beam is more accurate at sampling the characteristics of the film frame, and it also eliminates the possibility of burning, fading, stretching or otherwise marring the film. In fact, original camera negative can be transferred with little worry of wear and tear on most modern telecines.

Some films even use telecine as a final means of color correction. More advanced systems, such as the Phillips Spirit DataCine, can create digital files large enough to be stored and transferred back to film, eliminating the necessity of film negative color timing. In these instances, all of the final color correction is done in the telecine suite, not the lab.

THE COMPONENTS OF TELECINE

A modern telecine consists of three major components. A **film scanner**, the largest part of any telecine suite, is a machine on which the film is loaded. The film crosses the path of the scanner and each frame is accurately scanned and converted to video. The scanner can also read numeric information about the film, such as key numbers or bar codes, which will be discussed later. The method of scanning varies from model to model. The telecine scanner is remotely controlled, so by getting away from the telecine, sound noise is eliminated. Each scanner has a remote control keyboard located in the telecine suite.

The **color correction** system is also placed in the telecine suite. This is where the telecine operator, or colorist, can color correct and match each frame of film. The colorist corrects the color on individual frames and stores those parameters in a computer. Then, when the transfer is made to the tape, the coloring decisions that were stored are implemented in realtime as the film passes through the scanner.

The **telecine logger** keeps a log of activity in the telecine suite. Depending on the model and make of the logger, it can do as little as keeping a database of the relationship of the film frames to the videotape time code, or as much as memorizing settings of colorization, syncing audio to film and controlling the telecine transport. Some loggers also insert specific film & video information that goes direct to the videotape output of the telecine. This information is inserted either in the vertical interval of the video signal (which is not seen in the frame) or over the picture.

Many times the editor of a film will want information placed into the vertical interval of the telecined videotape. This information can include the film's edge code, audio time code, and video time code to ensure that the numbers in the editing database are consistent with the original telecine transfer. In order to do this, the assistant editor can ask to encode up to three lines of information into the vertical interval (VI) of the video signal. To use the VI information, a special reader that can display those numbers is required, because the vertical interval is not seen in the image on a video monitor. A drawback to this method is that some older NLEs do not digitize the telecine tape's vertical interval, eliminating the information encoded on the tape.

A visual burn-in on the picture is much more common and convenient. Because the video ultimately will not be the final source of a film, the numbers are placed over the picture, usually in the least obtrusive places. One of the most common schemes for a visual burn-in is to place the video time code on the bottom left of the frame; film key code, ink numbers, or 24 fps film time code in the right bottom of frame, and the audio time code in the top or upper left of the frame. For films with mattes, the burn-in is usually in the letterboxed area so that it does not interfere with the picture in any way (see Figure 3.3).

As the telecine session progresses, a database is created. The database records the relationship of the film frames to the video output. For example, the database may contain:

- Aaton code (Aaton 24 fps time code)
- Arri F/S (Arri 24 fps time code)
- Key Code™ (latent edge numbers)
- Acmade (ink numbers)
- Videotape time code
- DAT or Nagra time code (for Sound)

Once telecine is complete, the database can be output in a number of log formats, including:

- flex file
- FTL (film telecine log)
- OSC/R file
- Avid log exchange (ALE) files
- keylog files

And others. Without the database, it would be difficult to maintain continuity with the transferred videotape and the actual frames of the original film. Although there are always exceptions, negative cutters want an accurate list of edits based on the original film numbers.

METHODS OF TRANSFER

There are three methods of telecine transfer. In a **one light** transfer, also called a lab transfer, the colorist sets up for each reel of film on the first frame and colors it correctly, then lets the film play through, adjusting the colors and light from the transfer on the fly as the film passes through the telecine.

Why would anyone use such an inaccurate method of transferring film? Because it is the least expensive and therefore most common method of transferring dailies. As long as the editor can detect fine focus on the transfer and the luminance is good, it'll suffice for editing. And because the final product is film, not video from an NLE, one lights can save the production a lot of money.

But one lights have some drawbacks. It is possible that the colorization (or lack thereof) in one lights could cause the editor to pass over some potentially good footage. The lack of proper set up in a one light can create contrast and luminance variations that may hasten an editor's decision to choose a scene that is colored better, only because the colorist was able to adjust it more quickly as it went through the scanner. Film assistants can adjust the time-base corrector settings on the videotape recorder to compensate for this somewhat, but TBCs have a limited range of control, magnified by the limitations of videotape.

Best light transfer is a method of averaging the color set up of each shot across the entire roll. The colorist will set up on the first shot, then stop at each additional shot on the roll of film to find each scene's best light. What the colorist does NOT do is try to find continuity of colors between the shots. For example, with two different shots of the same set, the colorist will tweak each shot to look its best, but not necessarily to look the same as the other shots. Best lights are usually a little more expensive than one lights and are used on some films with medium or high budgets.

Scene-by-scene transfer is by far the most expensive. A supervised scene-by-scene transfer offers a precise color setup for each and every shot in the roll. A supervised transfer is just what it says it is— supervised, often by the director of the film, with a colorist tweaking according to the needs of the director. The continuity between scenes is carefully calibrated for uniformity. This method is prohibitively expensive as a means for producing a video master for offline nonlinear editing.

NTSC Telecine

The telecine scans each frame of film and then transfers it to videotape. But how does the film keep the timing consistent with videotape? Film runs at 24 frames per second. Video runs at 30 fps. To keep the proper timing of the film, that is, run the film at its original speed while recording to video at its native speed, it has to repeat some frames of the film on some fields of video. The process of repeating these frames, or actually holding them for an extra length of time, is called pulldown.

For every four frames of film, there is a need for five frames of video. But if every fourth frame of film was held for the duration of an extra frame of video, there would be a perceivable time lag or jutter in the picture, a sort of stopping and starting motion that occurred six times a second. And so, the engineers who developed telecine had to come up with a less perceivable yet precise way to maintain the 24 to 30 frame relationship.

An NTSC video picture consists of 525 lines of horizontal resolution. An electron gun scans the picture from top to bottom. When the gun scans the first field, it only scans the odd-numbered horizontal lines of the picture, then returns to the top. The second scan covers the even-numbered lines. Thus, a video frame actually consists of two separate components called fields. The two fields interlace with each other, and through persistence of vision, the viewer sees a single frame of video.

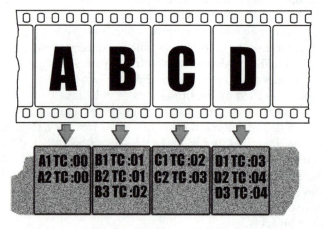

Figure 3.1   NTSC 2:3 pulldown

In order to smooth out the process and evenly distribute the pulldown, if every other frame of film for an extra field of video, it adds a total of one frame of video for every four frames of film. In other words, 30 frames of video is produced for every 24 frames of film. The process of holding the extra field every other frame is called 2:3 or 3:2 pulldown.

Here's how 2:3 pulldown precisely translates. The first frame of film, called the A frame, is held for two fields of video. The second frame of film, B frame, is held for three fields of video. The third frame, C, is held for only two fields of video, and finally, the D frame of film is held for three fields. This totals ten fields, which equals five frames of video for the A, B, C, and D frame of film. The equal spacing of the pulldown creates a perfect offset of fields; the process repeats itself 6 times per second. (The frame rate of video is actually 29.97. In order to compensate, telecines actually transfer the film at a speed of 23.976 fps.)

PAL Telecine

Film can be shot at 24 or 25 frames per second for PAL finishing and there are two ways to transfer PAL video.

PAL telecine A transfers frame for frame from the film to PAL video. A film shot at 24 or 25 fps can be transferred this way. If the film was shot and transferred at 25 fps, there is no modification in the play rate of the resulting videotape, because the frame rate is the same on both media. If the film was shot at 24 fps, it will play back 4.166% faster than it was originally shot when transferred to videotape. Using telecine A keeps the frame-to-frame ratio equal, but speeding up of the film can cause some problems. The 4.166% speed increase is not too noticeable visually but the sound also has to be sped up. It is only a half tone higher than normal, which works well with voices, but not particularly well for music. The process of speeding up the sound during transfer is relatively simple, as most modern DAT machines have the ability to play 6% faster or slower.

PAL telecine B transfers the film to video by adding a field every twelfth frame. Thus, a 24 fps film is translated to 25 fps of PAL video. An additional frame is generated to make one second of film equal to one second of video. Although the frame-to-frame ratio isn't equal, this method of transfer works fine for video output, and there's no need to speed up the sound.

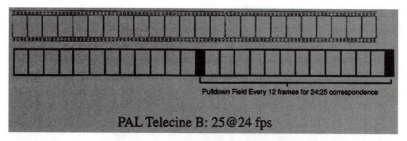

Figure 3.2   PAL telecine B pulldown

TELECINE CONSIDERATIONS

Before deciding which facility to use, the producer should make sure that the appropriate film to videotape transfer equipment is used. A telecine, not a film chain, should be used. A film chain is a video camera positioned in front of a film projection device and does not accurately measure pulldown. It may seem more economical at the outset, but using a film chain will cause more problems and work in the long run.

The editor should make sure that all of the film reference numbers run in ascending order. This seems only logical, but in some cases, a well-meant mistake can cause a multitude of problems. For example, when using certain types of camera devices for animation, the film is shot upside down and will need to be inverted later. A telecine operator could easily mistake the orientation of the film as reversed and transfer it upside down with descending numbers. It's up to the editor or assistant editor to make sure that the transfers are done correctly. Although some matchback programs can deal with descending key numbers, as a general rule, they don't. Telecine houses appreciate an immediate response; if a complaint is registered months later, it could be misconstrued as an effort to shave dollars off of the budget.

All transfers should be made with nondrop frame time code, preferably both in the vertical interval (VITC time code) and on the address track for longitudinal time code (LTC) with burn-in on the video signal area. Without time code, the database created in any NLE won't work. Nondrop frame is preferable, because a frame numbering scheme can be used to determine where an A frame is located. If nondrop frame time code were used with two field capture, the time code numbers would look something like those in Table 3.1

Table 3.1 Using Nondrop Frame Time Code in Telecine

Frame Fields	Corresponding NDF TC Frame
A/A	:00
B/B	:01
B/C	:02
C/D	:03
D/D	:04
A/A	:05

Using this method, the A frame occurs consistently on either the :00 or :05 frame. As a result, it is easy to find the A frame.

If drop frame is used, two frames are dropped at the end of every minute, excepting every tenth minute as shown in Table 3.2. As a result, the consistency is lost. This makes searching for A frames harder, which is important when working with 24 fps frame rates. Now the A frame is at an :05 time code and an :02 time code, and it will change for each minute that the frames were dropped. This causes a lot of confusion when trying to determine frames.

Table 3.2 Using Drop Frame Time Code With Telecine

Frame Fields	Corresponding DF TC Frame
A/A	:55
B/B	:56
B/C	:57
C/D	:58
D/D	:01
A/A	:02

It is also important, though not necessarily a telecine consideration, to record audio at 30 fps (not 29.97) with nondrop frame time code. Keeping the frame code mode consistent will help avoid mistakes down the line when conforming the film and making cut lists. It's also helpful when checking numbers in the frame of the burn-in windows. When a frame number drops in the audio time code and doesn't in the video time code, it seems confusing. Stick with nondrop and there will never be a reason to worry about it.

For every example, there is an exception. I have worked with films that use nothing more than visual orientation as a method of matching frames. It is not recommended that anyone use this type procedure, yet it is important to note that professionals have done it successfully. In David Barker's *Afraid of Everything*, the film, 35mm Eastman stock, was transferred without benefit of any key numbers in telecine. David assured us that we didn't need to ink the film, as his negative cutter would "eyeball" the neg. Because the film was shot at a low ratio and over a short period of time, his neg cutter was able to match it to the final video cut. So, although it is not a normal procedure, and certainly not taught in the classroom, it can be done.

Table 3.3   Telecine Options

Option	Description
Automated Telecine Log	Also known as a flex file or transfer log, the most common are.flx,.ftl and.ale files. The easiest way to get information in and out of the database. Otherwise, it will require recording information manually according to the burn-in windows, which aren't always reliable.
VITC	Vertical Interval Time Code. It's mandatory to have some kind of longitudinal (address track) time code on the videotape to maintain video-to-film frame relationships, but the vertical interval can also contain VITC, Aaton Code and key code numbers. Up to three lines of information can be recorded and later read using a vertical interval decoding device. These are great for maintaining burn-in information both on picture and in the vertical blanking signal of the videotape.
One Light Transfer Best Light Transfer Scene by Scene Transfer	The most economical of these is One Light. Even if the project finishes on video, a pull list can be created and a scene by scene transfer can be performed for only those items used in the film.
Time Logic Control (TLC)	TLC maintains the pulldown between stop and start points for the entire transfer. If the colorist stops telecine for a restart of the transfer, color adjustments or reel changes, the pulldown will continue as if uninterrupted at that edit point in the videotape.
A Frame White Flag	This creates a white flash in the vertical interval on the A frame of the videotape. It can be seen on an NTSC monitor when it is in underscan mode or by looking at the vertical interval. Also viewable if a waveform monitor is handy.
Hole Punch	Most camrolls are punched at the lab. A hole punch is added to an even frame at the head of the film before the first slate of the camera roll.
Burn-In Windows	One of the few controls to verify cut lists and EDLs. Key Numbers with pulldown and frame are normally bottom right, video time code is bottom left and audio time code is upper left.

TELECINE OPTIONS

Modern telecine facilities offer a variety of options that can help create and maintain the database information that will be necessary to integrate film with any NLE. Table 3.3 lists of some of the most commonly used options.

Figure 3.3   A typical videotape with burn-in windows.

Chapter 4:
Conforming a Workprint

Not all digital films are spared the blade. Although some can spend the entire phase of post production in the digital realm, most films can't escape the need for being screened in their natural environment: the theater. Rightly so, because one can never know what might be encountered until a film is displayed in the environment in which it was meant to be shown.

Not long ago I viewed a documentary about the building of Boeing's 777 aircraft. The engineers found a way to test the fitting of parts and structure of the plane in a simulated virtual mode. Nothing was ever manufactured, machined, or tested until it was first created and tested in a computer. Of course, eventually all parts were crafted and tested, and in the end, the plane had to be as airworthy in the real world as it was on the computer.

Conforming a workprint is like that. In the world of digital NLEs, the film is seen as it "will be". But one can only truly be sure of its effect when it is built in its final intended medium.

I've attended plenty of screenings of films that skipped conforming a workprint or bypassed screening in a larger format, like a projection TV. The final digital cut was output verbatim to a cut list and sent directly to the negative cutter. More often than not, there are problems with these films. Conforming a workprint gives editors an opportunity to correct problems. What is seen on the small screen doesn't always translate well to a theater, and vice versa. If a film were an aircraft, conforming a workprint would be its test flight.

The conforming process helps the people who handle the film later. In particular, it gives a road map for the negative cutter. Without a workprint, the neg cutter is working strictly with a list full of numbers. If any problems exist in the list, they might be discovered when it is too late. A workprint gives a direct physical frame-to-frame reference of the cut.

GETTING STARTED

Before the process of actually printing and cutting film begins, the editor needs to prepare the digital cut to match the characteristics of film. This can be a tedious process, but it also makes the difference between a well-done screening and a disastrous calamity of miscued reels. There are three steps that need to be taken.

Balance the cut into 1,000 foot reels
Add SMPTE leader
Create a pull list and an assemble list

Creating and Balancing the Reels

In the real world, 1,000 feet is the standard maximum length for any single reel of film intended for screening. The length of each individual reel can vary, depending on where the best cut point or ending is located. Normally, the best cut point is between scenes. At the end of each reel, another continuous second of the last scene on the reel is added after the last frame of action (LFOA). This LFOA (also called the EOR, end of reel, or LFOP, last frame of picture) is where the reel change should be made. The extra second is used for human error on the changeover between projectors. Some people, particularly those better versed in video than film, are shocked to learn that projection isn't a computerized science. More about that later.

Balancing can be tricky. The length of the reels will vary, but they should never be less than 700 feet nor more than 1,000 feet. When counting the footage, be sure to include the length of the SMPTE leader on each reel. It is preferable to keep the reel length longer than 800 feet, because anything less could lead to calamity in the projection room. An 800-foot roll of 35mm film is just under nine minutes long, and the projectionist needs time to load each reel.

There can be issues with measuring the lengths of film. Using an NLE that doesn't keep track of running footage during an edit necessitates the use of either a footage calculator or a chart (see Appendix A: Time/Footage Conversions). There is also a handy device used in many cutting rooms called a Reddy-Eddy. This device calculates footage and running time on a circular graph.

I use a footage calculator on my computer, but the length of reels can also be verified by some simple calculating.

For example, a reel of a 16mm feature ends at 23:40. The first step would be to translate everything into seconds. So take the number of minutes, multiply them by 60, and add them to the leftover seconds, like this:

$(23 * 60) + 40 = 1,420$ seconds

The next step is to take the total number of seconds and multiply them by 24 to determine the number of frames, like so:

$1,420 * 24 = 34,080$ frames

Finally, take the number of frames and divide them by the number of frames in a foot of film. In 16mm, this is normally 40 frames per foot. With 35mm, it would be 16 frames per foot. So the end result is:

34080 / 40 = 852 feet

852 feet is the length of the reel.

Figure 4.1   Measuring footage on the bench.

Adding SMPTE Leader on the NLE

Once manageable, balanced cut points for each reel are located, and separate sequences are made of the reels. In most NLEs it is very simple to mark the beginning and end frame and then drag them back as subcuts into a reel bin. After the subcuts for all of the reels are created, add SMPTE leader.

SMPTE leader can be added later when the reels are conformed and built, but I like to do it in the NLE first, because it's easier to calculate the length of each reel and create a continuity report, which documents the running time of each reel, before the pull list is created. The further I get ahead in my paperwork, the happier I am.

In order to create the complete reel in an NLE, SMPTE leader (on videotape) or a Quicktime movie of SMPTE leader is necessary. Once the SMPTE leader has been digitized, place it at the head of each reel in the NLE. The first frame should be the frame that has "Picture Start" on it. After the 2 frame, there should be 59 video frames of black, then the cut picture should begin.

Add one frame of 1000 Hz tone on the 2 frame. Like most facilities, we have a tone generator at Film Camp, but a 1000 Hz sound file can be imported into the NLE and cut on the 2 frame. This is called the 2 pop or sync pop.

Once the SMPTE has been added to all of the reels, output a cut list to go to the lab. The lab will create a roll of all of the scenes in the film. The next job is to cut them up and assemble them.

The Pull List

The pull list is a type of cut list that tells the person conforming exactly which shots to pull from an OCN or workprint. When a pull list is created, it lists the cuts by cam roll. That way, the person creating the workprint can pull everything needed from each roll, then print it. A pull list is the film world's equivalent to a video on-line C-mode editing list. If a standard **assemble** cut list, which lists the cuts chronologically from beginning to end, is used, the person conforming the film would have to go back and forth between cam rolls. This is not only unnecessary, but tedious.

Screenings can be pretty nervous gatherings, and every film cutter has an awful story to tell about a screening gone bad. Suffice it to say that accuracy is the key here. Put together a solid pull list for each reel and double check it. Some editors like to add extra frames called frame **handles** to each cut in the list. This can "force" them to double check the numbers when they assemble the workprint.

Every pull list should include

Lab roll number
Cam roll number
Scene number
Key number in
Key number out
Duration (feet + frames)

Anything else is optional. For most matchback and 24 fps NLE applications, master time code, comments, original clip names, and time code durations can be placed in the pull list as well. It's handy to have the time code durations to check against the digital cut, but not mandatory. After a pull list is made and checked, send it to the lab.

The lab can and will make mistakes from time to time. Once the workprint is received from the lab, check it against the pull list to make sure everything is there.

STARTING THE CONFORM

Once the workprint is made, it's time to conform. If the editor absolutely feels uncomfortable with physically cutting film for the first time, he or she can always hire an experienced assistant to do it for them. But if someone else does the cutting, it's important to watch carefully and ask lots of questions.

Figure 4.2   Cutting on the frameline

Most film editors love touching film. But that's not necessarily true for those of us who work mostly with video. At first, one might feel overcautious. In this case, fear is good. Make sure the print is conformed right the first time, or it will be tough putting it back together.

The first step is to separate each shot in the pull list and hang it in a bin. Handle the workprint carefully and make sure it stays put on its bin hook. It's very easy to scratch work print. Normally a director might expect the print to be pretty scuffed up by the time it makes it to a screening, but when used in conjunction with an NLE, expectations run higher, as the workprint is new.

On the edit bench, load the first roll of workprint on the left-hand side, shiny side down, emulsion up. Zip past the leader and find the first frame of print. Check the key number against the pull list. To count frames, find the nearest key number. There is a small dot in between the key number and key code (bar code) on the edge of the film next to the sprocket holes. This is the zero frame reference mark (see Figure 4.3). The zero frame reference mark lies next to the "Zero" frame. From that mark, count frames. Each corresponding frame beyond the mark is +1,

+2 and so on. Find the proper frame and insert it into the splicer. The cut should be made along the frameline before the frame. Once the film is aligned into the sprockets of the splicer and it is verified that the blade will fall on the frameline, cut it.

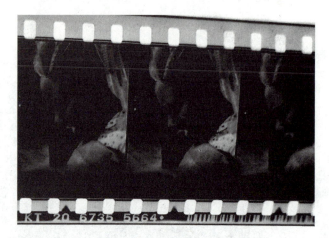

Figure 4.3   The zero frame reference mark next to the key number

Pull the first frame of the clip to the takeup reel on the right side of the bench and zip ahead to the last frame of the clip according to the pull list. Remember to count forward from the key number. Be sure to make the cut after the correct frame.

As each clip is cut out of the roll of workprint, place a trim tab on it and hang it in the bin on a pin. A trim tab contains information relating to each clip. There are two types of trim tabs: rectangular (West Coast) and cross shaped (East Coast). The trim tabs contain information helpful in identifying the clip. Typically, a trim tab can contain key numbers, in and out; a description of the shot (i.e., "LS- Gilligan and Mary Ann"); and scene and take number.

As each clip is cut, hang it in the bin left to right to match the order in which the clips will be conformed, using an assemble list as a guide. Hang each shot on a separate pin. Once all of the workprint is hung in the bin, the fun really begins.

Splicing It Together

Before splicing the reels together, the first task is to output an assemble list for each reel. If SMPTE leader was added in the NLE sequence, it will be the first cut. From there, take each clip in the list and add it to the reel. The cuts in the assemble list should be in chronological order according to the original digital version of the reel. A splicer and plenty of tape are needed for this task. For a screening, I highly recommend that both sides of the splice are taped. If the film is being screened on a flatbed or upright, taping one side should be enough.

Figure 4.4   A West Coast trim tab

Eventually, every editor associated with film will need to learn how to properly use a splicer. It takes time, patience, and a little manual dexterity. Explaining how to splice takes little effort: just cut, tape, and tamp it down. But the best method of learning how to use a splicer is to work with someone who has used it before. Once the process is learned, splicing is like riding a bike.

There are many different splicers on the market. One of the most popular is the Rivas. Rivas splicers, also known as butt splicers, have sprockets for alignment, straight and slanted channel cutting guides, two tape dispensers, a large blade, and a tamper for securing the tape (see Figure 4.5).

There are two types of tape: clear and white. White tape is used for sound, clear for picture. Pictures are cut straight across the frameline. Sound is cut diagonally.

Film reels use three types of leader: clear leader for head and tail, picture leader for information at head and tail, and SMPTE leader at the beginning just before the picture starts. To begin, some clear leader is needed. It takes 10 to 12 feet of leader to thread a projector. The clear leader takes a beating during rewinding, so several feet won't hurt. After the clear leader, add some picture leader. On the picture leader, write information about the reel with a black permanent marker. For example:

"GOOD TASTE TAKES A HOLIDAY" CUT WORK   PIX   R-1   PIX HEADS.

A consistent rule is that picture tracks are marked with black markers and sound is marked with red.

After the picture leader, splice in the SMPTE leader. Order this from the lab if necessary. As splicing tape is added to each cut, make sure that the tamper is pressed hard against the tape surface to ensure a firm splice.

Figure 4.5   A Rivas Splicer

From here, begin the picture conform. Follow the assemble list from beginning to end for each reel. In the original digital cut, 24 frames should have been remaining at the end for a changeover between reels. After the changeover, attach a picture tail leader and several feet of clear leader.

Opticals

When blending any two film elements together or manipulating the frame of a film, such as in a dissolve, a matte, a fade or a blow-up of the frame, an optical is required. Opticals are almost never created for screenings. If there are any opticals in the cut list, it is necessary to add leader for the duration of those opticals. Some editors use "scene missing" leader for these sections. Others attach white leader. But be sure that the leader is the correct duration for the optical in order to keep the reel in sync with sound.

Another method for dealing with opticals involves the cut list. If the option of showing dissolves and wipes as cuts is selected, the two shots can be spliced together and the transition can be drawn with a grease pencil. With this method, it clearly shows that there is a transition, but it also doesn't interrupt the flow of the film as it is screened.

Marking Workprint for Motor Start and Changeover

Every motion picture contains two marks at the end of the reel. These marks can be seen in the upper right-hand corner of the picture. The first is called a motor start cue. This signals the projectionist to start the motor (but not the projector lamp and sound head) for the next reel. The second is a changeover cue. This signals the projectionist to switch between projectors to the next reel of film.

Many modern theaters have huge platters where the entire film is laid and projected from beginning to end. The projectionist hits one button and the film begins. But this isn't true for all theaters and most screening rooms. These rooms use two projectors in the booth and switch projectors during reel changes or changeovers. In order to let the projectionist know when to change reels, a visual cue is given in the picture on the screen.

Some assistants use small, sticky, white dots and others mark the workprint with the slash of a grease pencil. For a screening, either is fine. Each cue consists of four marked frames. It's important that the marks made are visible on the screen, so don't forget to mark it within the aspect area of the film.

The motor cue begins 200 frames before the last frame of action (LFOA). Beginning at that point, mark four consecutive frames, again considering the screening aspect of the film.

The changeover cue occurs one second before the LFOA. Remember, an additional second of picture is necessary beyond the LFOA for human error. Mark four consecutive frames from the one-second point.

Figure 4.6   Marking the 2 pop in the sync blocks

Sound

When it comes to NLEs, sound is relatively simple to output. Sound can be transferred directly from NLE to time code DAT or other time coded source. In fact, time coded source isn't really necessary, so long as the 2 pop is inserted at the correct point.

Some editors take a little time to create a rough mix for screenings. In better-funded films, the rough sound would go to the sound department for a temp mix. Either way, anything that will enhance the screening process is considered good.

Sound can be transferred digitally direct from NLE to a tape source. Be sure to transfer at the proper sampling rate. If there is access to direct digital output from the NLE and input to the source, use it. The fidelity and clarity make a big difference at screenings.

From the taped output, the sound will have to be transferred to mag stock. But before it is transferred, there is one small issue to resolve. If the NLE cut picture and sound are at a true 24fps rate, it's fine. But if matchback software was used and the pulldown speed wasn't corrected, the difference in speed will need to be resolved.

Chapter 2 discusses slowing down telecine to match the NTSC frame rate of 29.97. To match the video frame rate, film is actually transferred via telecine at 23.976 fps instead of 24. As a result, because the speed of sound on matchback projects wasn't properly adjusted with an audio coprocessor, the resulting output will run at 23.976, not 24. This means that the sound is running about .01% too slow. When the sound output is sent out for a mag stock transfer, be sure to make a note to the lab that the sound needs to be sped up .01% during transfer.

After the sound is transferred, there is the final task of building the sound reels. Because the mag in is one piece, there will be no need for internal edits. But clear leader and marked sound leader need to be added at head and tail of each reel. Use the same pattern that was shown for the picture leader, but use a red marker instead of black. The 2 pop needs to be marked with a red marker so that the projectionist can set it up appropriately to ensure that sound will run in sync with picture (see Figure 4.6).

Continuity Reports

Once the reels are built, it's time to make a reel breakdown or continuity report. The report shows the scene numbers on each reel, footage length and time. At the bottom, there is space for total footage and duration.

film camp

REEL CONTINUITY REPORT

DATE **12/19/00**

REEL	SCENES	LENGTH	TIME
1	1 – 8	949+01	10:32:21
2	9 – 21	972+13	10:48:16
3	21 – 29	862+13	9:35:06
4	30 – 45	937+11	10:25:04
5	46 – 57	944+05	10:29:16
6	57 – 65	889+04	9:52:15
7	66 – 74	980+15	10:53:29
8	75 – 89	906+12	10:04:15
9	90 – 112	764+07	8:29:19
10			
11			
12			
13			
14			
15			
TOTAL		8206+01	91:10:21

Figure 4.7   Continuity Report

Chapter 5:
Cut Lists

A cut list is a printed version of the edit decisions. It contains key or ink numbers, time code from the master videotape edit, and information about the original camera and sound rolls used in the cut. Cut lists are normally used for picture only, unless the audio is transferred to mag stock and ink numbered. For audio, an edit decision list (EDL) is assembled using SMPTE time code as a reference. There are two common reasons to create a cut list: to conform a workprint, or to send to a negative cutter.

NEGATIVE CUTTERS

If the editor is not experienced at negative cutting, he or she will have to send a cut list out to another person. One of the basic principals of working on a motion picture is that if something goes out, it must have paperwork, and lots of it. Be sure to include as much information as possible for a neg cutter when sending out your cut list. This can include a digital cut of the edit on a videotape for confirming the cut points, reel continuity reports, editing notes, and so on. The more information the neg cutter receives, the more likely he or she will be to accurately recreate your edits. An editor should never assume that a neg cutter knows how he or she works.

A less often used but far more sensible approach is to actually call or even visit the neg cutter before the goods are delivered. It isn't always possible, because the neg cutter may be in another city or even a different country, but even an email is good. Get to know this person. Know how the neg cutter works, what his or her preferences are and how they intend to complete the incredible task of finishing the film. Creating dialog with the neg cutter does two things for the film: it shows the neg cutter that you're not just another pretty negative and it emphasizes the understanding of the importance of their role.

Okay, I can hear some of you laughing. But everyone needs a pat on the back now and then, right? Why not show a little attention to the most important person on your film? Remember, the hand that cuts the OCN is the hand that rules the world! Neg cutting is a thankless and unforgiving job. This person is required to properly perform physically all of the cuts completed on the NLE. One false slip and POW! The film is ruined. If the neg cutter seems nervous, that's probably a good sign.

TYPES OF CUT LIST

There are several different types of cut list, each of these lists corresponds to a particular need of a film.

The Assemble List

The assemble list, also known as a cut list, is a list of the cuts made on the film in the order in which they will be assembled. It starts with the first cut and ends with the last. Assemble lists can be customized to include several bits of information, depending on the software used to generate the list. At a bare minimum, every assemble list needs the following:

> Starting key number
> Ending key number
> Duration (feet + frames)
> Time code in (from the video master)
> Time code duration
> Camera roll
> Scene and take

I like to include just about everything possible in my lists in order to minimize mistakes. Those things can include a description of the cut and any comments added during post production. These things are all important to me if I am using the cut list to conform a workprint.

Frame Handles

When the software is set up to output an assemble list, notice that there is an entry for "handles." The handles for a cut list are the numbers of additional frames of film required to make a cut. If a workprint is being conformed, no handles are necessary. The frame is cut in between frames and will not overlap to any additional frames. However, if the list is being sent to a neg cutter, check to see how many frames they'll need as handles. Most neg splicers require at least a single frame. I've dealt with some neg cutters who request as many as three extra frames on each side of the cut.

```
Avid Cut Lists                      created at 18:20:39 Thu 11 Jan 2001
Project: JB
List Title: ASSEMBLE LIST

ASSEMBLE LIST                    11 events      handles = -1
Picture 1                         2 dupes       total footage:    19+12
Assemble List                     0 opticals    total time: 00:00:13:04
----------------------------------------------------------------------------
        Footage   Duration     First/Last Key    Cam Roll   Sc/Tk   Clip Name

  1.    2342+05    2+15   KZ 61 0970-6578+04       003     2mos/12  Airport      Dupe
        2345+03                      6581+02                                     Set #1

  2.    2345+04    2+15   KZ 61 0970-6578+04       003     2mos/12  Airport      Dupe
        2348+02                      6581+02                                     Set #1

  3.    2348+03    2+11   KZ 61 0970-6598+05       003     2mos/12  Airport
        2350+13                      6600+15

  4.    2350+14    0+15   KZ 69 0721-8630+04       001      4a/6    Restaurant
        2351+12                      8631+02

  5.    2351+13    0+07   KZ 69 0721-8626+13       001      4a/6    Restaurant
        2352+03                      8627+03

  6.    2352+04    1+06   KZ 69 0653-8071+03       002      6cu/9   Mad Dog      Dupe
        2353+09                      8072+08                                     Set #2

  7.    2353+10    1+06   KZ 69 0653-8071+03       002      6cu/9   Mad Dog      Dupe
        2354+15                      8072+08                                     Set #2

  8.    2355+00    1+15   KZ 61 0970-6578+04       003     2mos/12  Airport      Dupe
        2356+14                      6580+02                  .                  Set #1

  9.    2356+15    1+15   KZ 61 0970-6594+06       003     2mos/12  Airport
        2358+13                      6596+04

 10.    2358+14    1+04   KZ 61 0970-6582+02       003     2mos/12  Airport
        2360+01                      6583+05

 11.    2360+02    1+15   KZ 69 0721-8632+02       001      4a/6    Restaurant
        2362+00                      8634+00

(end of Assemble List)
ASSEMBLE LIST                    11 events      handles = -1
Track 1                           2 dupes       total footage:    19+12
```

Figure 5.1 An assemble list

Why are handles so important? Neg cutters often use splicers that cut through the center of the next adjacent frame to the cut. If that next frame is needed elsewhere, they need to know that a duplicate is necessary before the cut is performed. Otherwise, the frame will be cut in half, rendering it unusable.

The Dupe List

If there is any repetition of footage in a film or handles that overlap in the assemble list, a dupe list is mandatory. For a neg cutter, the dupe list is the first order of business. The neg cutter sends the neg to the lab to duplicate any frames that are used. A dupe list should be created even if the editor believes that there are no dupes in the picture. Remember, there is no such thing as "oops" in the world of neg cutting. A dupe list typically consists of the starting key number, ending key number, duration (feet + frames), time code in (from the video master), time code duration, camera roll, and scene and take. Other items can be added as well, depending on what the software permits.

```
Avid Cut Lists                        created at 18:03:31 Thu 11 Jan 2001
Project: JB
List Title: ASSEMBLE LIST

ASSEMBLE LIST                   2 groups        handles = 0
Picture 1
Dupe List
---------------------------------------------------------------------------------
Group  Num  Footage   Duration      First/Last Key    Cam Roll   Sc/Tk   Clip Name
---------------------------------------------------------------------------------

  1.                   2+15   (total)                     003     2mos/12  Airport

       1.   2342+05    2+15   KZ 61 0970-6578+04
            2345+03                       6581+02

       2.   2355+00    1+15   KZ 61 0970-6578+04
            2356+14                       6580+02

       3.   2345+04    2+15   KZ 61 0970-6578+04
            2348+02                       6581+02

---------------------------------------------------------------------------------

  2.                   1+06   (total)                     002     6cu/9    Mad Dog

       1.   2352+04    1+06   KZ 69 0653-8071+03
            2353+09                       8072+08

       2.   2353+10    1+06   KZ 69 0653-8071+03
            2354+15                       8072+08

(end of Dupe List)
ASSEMBLE LIST                   2 groups        handles = 0
Track 1
Dupe List
---------------------------------------------------------------
Group  Num  Footage   Duration    Sc/Tk    Clip Name
---------------------------------------------------------------

  1.                   2+15   (total)
                              2mos/12  Airport

       1.   2345+04    2+15
            2348+02

       2.   2355+00    1+15
```

Figure 5.2   A dupe list

The Optical List

The next list is called an optical list. Here we enter the world of **A/B strand conforming**. Here's a rule of thumb: if the film is 35mm, it is almost always an A strand conform. If it is 16mm, it can be conformed A/B.

The advantage of A/B strand conforming is that the film can use two strands to be conformed. In other words, optical prints of certain dissolves can be avoided by merging the two strands. For example, in the case of a dissolve, the lab can print it by irising down the camera on the "from" source on strand A while irising up the "to" source on strand B incrementally. In order for this to happen, the dissolves must be **lab standard durations**. Lab standard dissolves normally include durations of 16, 24, 32, 48, 64, and 96 frames. Any other length will have to go to an optical printer. I mention this because optical printing is very expensive. Many inexperienced indie directors appreciate this little tidbit. Changing some of the dissolve durations by a few frames can make all the difference in the world to the budget.

Table 5.1   Lab standard dissolves

Duration	Film Frames	NTSC frames	PAL Frames
2/3 second	16 frames	20 frames	17 frames
1 second	24 frames	30 frames	25 frames
1 1/3 seconds	32 frames	40 frames	33 frames
2 seconds	48 frames	60 frames	50 frames
2 2/3 seconds	64 frames	80 frames	67 frames
4 seconds	96 frames	120 frames	100 frames

Standard opticals are dissolves, fade-ins, fade-outs and superimpositions. Fade ins and fade outs are also A/B strand capable at lab standard durations. Again, any other duration would make the fade an optical. Superimpositions are different, however. A superimposition, unlike a dissolve, mixes between two sources and holds the mixed image for a duration, before either cutting away or fading out one or both sources.

Titles from any NLE will have to be made by a titles or opticals company, unless the project is a DV film. Even then it is recommended, due to resolution limitations of video, that an optical be created. Even in the case of DV to film, a title over black would be better produced as a separate film optical.

A typical optical list will show key start and end numbers for the from and to sources, with a frame count for the duration. Many neg and workprint cutters prefer an optical list format called optical blocks. The block format makes it easier to identify the from and to sources, with the from source on the top portion of the block and the to source at the bottom. By using a geometric shape, it is easier to identify which is which at a glance, rather than poring through the list to verify the information.

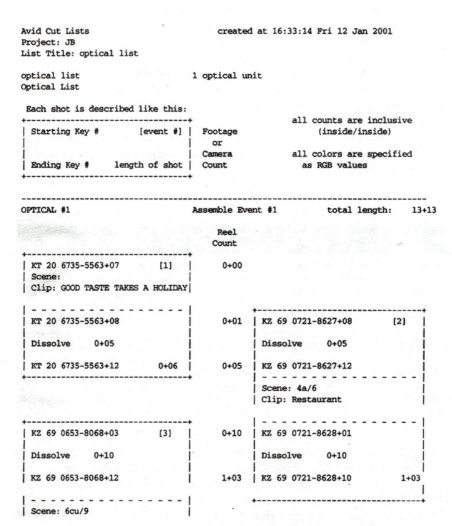

```
Avid Cut Lists                          created at 16:33:14 Fri 12 Jan 2001
Project: JB
List Title: optical list

optical list                     1 optical unit
Optical List

Each shot is described like this:
+-----------------------------------+           all counts are inclusive
| Starting Key #          [event #] | Footage             (inside/inside)
|                                   | or
|                                   | Camera      all colors are specified
| Ending Key #      length of shot  | Count               as RGB values
+-----------------------------------+


----------------------------------------------------------------------------
OPTICAL #1                           Assemble Event #1      total length:  13+13

                                         Reel
                                         Count

+-----------------------------------+
| KT 20 6735-5563+07          [1]   |    0+00
| Scene:                            |
| Clip: GOOD TASTE TAKES A HOLIDAY  |

|  - - - - - - - - - - - - - -  |             +-----------------------------------+
| KT 20 6735-5563+08            |    0+01     | KZ 69 0721-8627+08          [2]   |
|                               |             |                                   |
| Dissolve      0+05            |             | Dissolve        0+05              |
|                               |             |                                   |
| KT 20 6735-5563+12    0+06    |    0+05     | KZ 69 0721-8627+12                |
+-------------------------------+             |  - - - - - - - - - - - - - - - -  |
                                              | Scene: 4a/6                       |
                                              | Clip: Restaurant                  |

+-------------------------------+             |  - - - - - - - - - - - - - - - -  |
| KZ 69 0653-8068+03    [3]     |    0+10     | KZ 69 0721-8628+01                |
|                               |             |                                   |
| Dissolve      0+10            |             | Dissolve        0+10              |
|                               |             |                                   |
| KZ 69 0653-8068+12            |    1+03     | KZ 69 0721-8628+10      1+03      |
                                              +-----------------------------------+
|  - - - - - - - - - - - - - -  |
| Scene: 6cu/9                  |
```

Figure 5.3   An optical list configured with optical blocks

Now that we've described the list, here is a warning: find an optical house that does excellent work. It's easy to go with a low bidder and report to the director that the budget is saved. But a bad optical can be disastrous. If you've never done opticals before, consult with other editors and assistants, your lab, and your neg cutter. They know someone who can do a good job at a reasonable price.

The Pull List

The final type of cut list is called a pull list. Pull lists make it easy to conform both workprint and negative. The pull list will show the cuts in the film arranged in the order of the reel from which they originated, so that the person conforming can "pull" the clips. It is normally sorted by cam roll and then from lowest to highest key numbers so that the selections are cut incrementally, rather than having to go back and forth on each cam roll.

There are alternative types of pull lists as well. A scene pull list shows cuts arranged first in the order of scene, then arranged by their associated cam roll numbers. This list is very similar to a scene assemble list, which has the cuts sorted by where they first appeared in the assemble list.

Lok Box

Before sending a list to the neg cutter, you'll probably want to also send a **lok box** video. A lok box is a digital cut or output of the film on tape connected to a film gang synchronizer. Before creating a lok box, separate the cut into built reels, as described in Chapter 4. It is advisable to put a time code burn-in on the tape of record master time code in addition to any other burn-ins that are already there. This makes it easier for the neg cutter to gauge duration.

The Avid Film Composer offers a very desirable option for neg cutters: a lok box output that is frame-for-frame accurate. This type of output prints only film frames to the tape, with no pulldown. The result, when played at normal speed, is cartoon like sound, because the picture is speeded up- no pulldown is added to create thirty frames from the original twenty-four frames. The advantage of this frame-accurate output is that the neg cutter can jog through it and get an accurate accounting of each frame.

Conformed Workprint

Although a lok box video is an adequate visual representation of the film, nothing works better than a conformed workprint. The frame-for-frame accuracy and synchronized sound answer any questions that a neg cutter might have. Although it's more expensive and time consuming, a conformed workprint not only tells the neg cutter the numbers, but shows them the numbers, complete with grease pencil and red audio markings. It's more difficult to mistake intentions when a positive of the film is already assembled for reference.

When sending the lists to a neg cutter, be sure of two things. First, discuss the project with the neg cutter in full, learn all of his/her needs and output lists that conform to the neg cutter's way of working. Second, have a phone nearby. If there are any questions, they'll need to be answered immediately. Between the cut lists, a lok box, and a conformed workprint, the neg cutter should have all she or he needs. But there are occasions when questions come up. Availability is important in order to expedite the neg cutting process.

Chapter 6:
24 fps versus Matchback

Before integrating a project with an NLE, a working frame rate must be determined. In the NTSC world, there are two: 24 fps and 30 fps. For PAL video, you'll need to determine whether you're going to work with Telecine A without pulldown, where the film is shot at 24 or 25 fps and is telecined at 25 fps; or with Telecine B, where the film is shot at 24 fps and is telecined at 24 fps with two fields of pulldown to equal 25 frames per second. If you choose to work at 30 fps or use Telecine B, you're going to need software that can compute the matchback of your edits to the native film frame rate.

In this chapter, we'll look at the differences between native 24 and 30 fps matchback projects as well as those PAL projects using pulldown versus speeded up transfer. We'll examine some of the problems associated with each and also the advantages of working with them.

NTSC: 24 fps Projects

A true 24 fps project has a direct frame to frame correspondence with the film. There are no pulldown fields and therefore, what you see is what you get. NLEs and film software applications use one of two methods to create 24 fps projects.

They remove the pulldown fields during digitization.
They remove the pulldown fields after digitization.

Working at 24 fps can be problematic, especially if it's not clear where the A frame is located. As discussed in Chapter 3, it is important that the telecine facility records the A frame on a :00 frame of a nondrop frame time coded videotape. Identification of the A frame is important to the software, because it will have to determine where the pulldown fields are located in order to ignore them. If the wrong frame is identified, the result will be a picture with jerky action, because the wrong two fields will be removed for each cycle of frames. For example, if the B frame was mistakenly identified to the NLE as an A frame, it would ignore the first field of frame 3 (which would be a D frame) and also ignore the last field of frame 5, which would be an A frame. The removal of these two fields would produce a jitter in any camera motion or action within the frame. If this mistake of misidentification is made, it's necessary to unlink the media (on an Avid), delete it, and redigitize it with the proper frame identification.

There are some new products that have come along recently that depend on nondrop frame time code for proper identification. These video capture cards, which remove pulldown or perform a **reverse telecine**, use the time code to determine which pulldown fields to remove. As a result, they can ease some of the workload. However, if there are any anomalies in the telecine transfer, it goes back to the hard and tried way of manual identification and digitization. How well this digitization will go over with the film crowd remains to be seen.

When the telecine log is accurate and the numbers in the burn-ins match what is seen in the database, a 24 fps project is all but unbreakable. The great advantage is that there is frame-to-frame correspondence and no worries about adding or subtracting frames, as in matchback situations. Fast montages and flash cuts won't pose a problem, because all of the key numbers are in the database.

NTSC Matchback

Matchback software programs were initially created to deal with projects created at 30 fps. More recently, some of these programs have added software-based reverse telecine and 24 fps capabilities. Newer video capture cards can remove pulldown and work in conjunction with matchback applications such as Film-Logic to create a true 24 fps cut list.

The problems associated with matchback are simple: there are two different frame rates, thus a single frame is added for every four frames from the original film, so the trouble is editing with pulled down frames. But pulldown isn't the only consideration. Differences in frame rate can create problems of their own. The time base between the two mediums is different, so short edits will inevitably pose time base problems. Consider this: if several single frame edits are made using several A frames of a telecine transfer as a source, matchback will have to trim back the edit. The A frame is normally the start of a pulldown cycle. It consists of two fields, both with the same time code. So if 30 single-frame edits were made with A frames, 30 frames equals 1 second of video. But 30 frames equal 1.25 seconds of film. The matchback software will have to trim off six single-frame edits when creating a cut list for film to make the duration of the sequence correct.

Almost all matchback software makes adjustments from the tail of an edit, when an inaccuracy in duration is detected. In the case of these thirty single-frame edits, every fifth edit would be cut to maintain time consistency. This time base error is commonly referred to as matchback running long. Although it is uncommon, it can happen in a unique situation such as the one described in Figure 6.1.

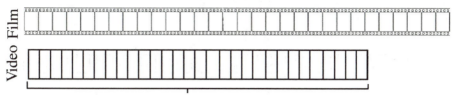

For Every 30 frames of video, there are 24 frames of film.

Matchback Running Long: Time Base Error

Problem: If 30 "A" frames were cut together in a flash montage, the matchback would normally run 1.25 seconds because of the time base difference between film and video. Therefore, matchback will have to "lose" 6 frames. But which 6 frames?

Figure 6.1   Matchback Running Long

Matchback software can also run short. Consider the same situation, except that instead of using A frames, use B frames. In a film transfer, the B frame lasts for three fields, covering the two fields of the second video frame and the first field of the third video frame in the pulldown cycle. So if 30 B frames were edited together as a 60-frame sequence, the matchback software would compute this as a 30 film frame edit, because the B frame consists of two different frames of video, but only one frame of film. Instead of listing 48 frames of film in the list, it would list 30 frames, or 1.25 seconds of film. As a result the matchback software must again determine how to create the same duration, this time by adding film frames. In this case, thirty film frames would be the equivalent of 1.25 seconds. An additional 18 frames of film would need to be added to the sequence in order to maintain time consistency.

Although these two examples are extreme, they illustrate why a matchback system can never be quite frame accurate. Matchback software will add or subtract a frame at the end of each edit to retain the proper duration of the film in proportion with the video. But because the editor cuts on a 30 fps system, matchback will occasionally have to adjust some edits, which could be a problem.

The way to avoid any frame issues when using matchback would be to cut in on an A frame and out on a D frame for every edit. Hardly a practical solution!

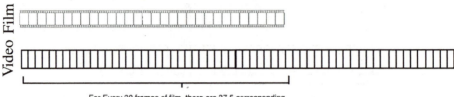

For Every 30 frames of film, there are 37.5 corresponding frames of video.

Matchback Running Short: Pulldown Error

Problem: If 60 "B" frames were cut together in 2 frame edits, the matchback would normally run1.25 seconds if there was a direct frame to frame correspondence because of the extra pulldown "B" frame in a matchback project.

Figure 6.2   Matchback Running Short

PAL 25 at 24 fps Projects (Telecine B)

PAL projects that are shot and transferred at 24 fps to PAL videotape require a single frame of pulldown to equal the 25 fps rate of PAL video. As discussed in Chapter 3, this is known as Telecine B. Telecine B does not work with all matchback applications, but Slingshot's 24:25 preference allows for Telecine B, as does FilmLogic, which can match back the list accordingly.

The artifacts of matchback with Telecine B are less significant because of the lesser occurrence of pulldown. With NTSC matchback, there is a 50 percent chance that the last frame of a cut will need to be timed forward or backward, because of the four frames— A, B, C, and D —two of them contain a field of pulldown. With Telecine B, the occurrence of pulldown is less common. As a result, there is an 8 percent chance that pulldown could affect matchback with a PAL telecine B list.

If a model similar to NTSC's frame count is used, the J frame would be the pulldown frame. As a result, if several J frames were edited together in the video, each representing two frames, matchback could again run short, as with NTSC.

Running long would be different however, because the maximum difference would be a miscount of 4.133 percent, the time base difference between 24 fps and 25 fps. For example, if any 50 single frames of PAL video were edited as single-frame cuts, only two frames would need to be cut to maintain time consistency. Although the problem is similar to that of NTSC, it is not nearly as disastrous and the fix is simpler.

1:1 PAL Frame Correspondence (Telecine A)

Although telecine A presents significant problems for editors with relation to the speeded up picture and sound, there is no need for matchback due to the fact that there is a 1:1 frame correspondence. But like the .01 percent pulldown issues associated with a 24fps NTSC project, there are going to be sound speed issues.

PAL Sound and Picture Digitized Together

Some software offers solutions that simplify the matter. For example, Avid's Film Composer has solutions for 24 or 25 fps projects transferred at 24 fps with sound. For projects shot at 24 fps but digitized at 25 to create a 1:1 ratio, the film is digitized in the normal way and the Avid will slow it back down to its native 24 fps frame rate. There is no need to adjust any pulldown settings on the hardware. In fact, doing so would mess up the project. By selecting 24 fps as the project speed, the Avid knows that the film was shot at this rate and slows it down. This also slows down the audio transferred with the film, and the sampling rate will drop at the same 4.166 percent ratio. So, for a 44.1kHz sampling rate, the result is a 42.33kHz sample.

PAL Sound and Picture Digitized Separately

When picture and sound are digitized separately, the picture can be slowed down using Avid's film settings preferences. Select a 24 fps speed and the film will slow down appropriately. Sound will be digitized and remain at production speed with no sampling issues. A digital cut can be performed with either pulldown inserted much like telecine B processes or with the picture and sound sped up 4.166 percent for a 1:1 frame ratio on the final video.

Telecine A can also be achieved with Final Cut Pro by slowing down the clips by 4.166 percent. This can be done for sound or picture and is easily attained. However, doing this will cause the time code numbers to increase according to the existing frame rate. A project telecined at 25 fps can be digitized and edited in that mode, then output it as a separate sequence with the time base adjusted. But you'll want to duplicate the sequence for proper matchback prior to doing this.

A Final Note

The decision whether or not to use matchback versus 24 fps projects should depend on the support staff. If there aren't enough eyes checking numbers, pulldown and sound speeds, a matchback would be more convenient. However, if a frame-to-frame correspondence between your media and the original film is required, 24 fps and telecine A are the only way to go.

Chapter 7:
Editing Film on
Avid NLEs
with FilmScribe

Avid's FilmScribe™ software is integrated with Media Composer or Xpress software and does not require separate databasing of telecine information outside of the NLE application. Telecine logs are imported directly into the Avid bins after conversion to the Avid Log Exchange (ALE) format. The information from the logs is stored in the Avid bins and doesn't require further conversion to create a cut list.

Avid makes NLEs in both NT and Mac flavors. The instructions in this chapter work for both platforms. but I use the more common Mac systems in the examples. Whenever *Command* is mentioned, NT users should use *Control*, and whenever *Option* is mentioned, NT users should use *Alt*.

CONVERTING TELECINE FILES

The process begins with the conversion of telecine logs to Avid Log Exchange format. Avid Log Exchange isn't a telecine log format, but it is widely used as a conversion tool. Many telecine databases can now output in ALE format, eliminating the need for this procedure.

Telecine logs are primarily in one of three formats: **flex files**, **Evertz files** or **Aaton files**. Any of these formats can be converted to ALE format using the Avid Log Exchange application. The ALE application comes bundled with Film Composer but is not serialized or copy protected by Avid. I suppose this was done to promote wider use of the format. The strategy succeeded, because ALE is commonly used in almost all log conversion and matchback applications. The Avid Log Exchange program is normally found in the Utilities folder of Media Composer or Xpress. Frequent users of ALE put an alias or shortcut to the program on their desktop. When the application is launched, a window opens with two columns, one for input format, the other for output. When converting to an Avid usable format, the output should be ALE. For input, several different formats can be selected. There is also a selection for Automatic. This is the easiest method of running the program. When Automatic is selected, ALE determines which format the file was created in by reading its file extension. In Table 7.1, all of the acceptable telecine log formats for ALE are shown, along with their file extensions. ALE can output logs in the formats shown in Table 7.2.

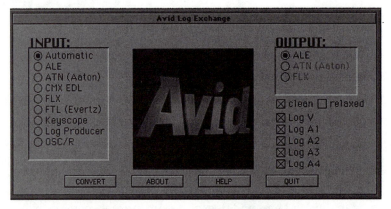

Figure 7.1 Avid Log Exchange Interface

After ALE has been set up, quit the program and drag and drop telecine log files onto the icon or alias for automatic conversion. In order to preserve the original logs, it is strongly suggested that the log is copied from its original media (normally a floppy or Zip disk) to a folder on the desktop. In this way, it ensures that the original data won't be corrupted, lost, or destroyed. Another reason to copy the logs is that ALE will place converted logs onto their originating volume. If it's a floppy disk and the disk is full, it won't convert them. Instead, it will return a Disk Full error.

SETTING UP THE PROJECT

Now that the files have been converted to an Avid readable format, it's time to bring them into the project. But first, a project must be created.

File Type	Extension
Aaton	.flx or agxxx.Txx
CMX	.cmx
EditDroid	.log
Evertz	.ftl
Flex	.flx
Quantel Harry	.vtr
Keyscope	.ksl
Log Producer	.llp
OSC/R	.asc
Skycode	.ale

Table 7.1   ALE Import Formats

File Type	Extension
Avid Log Exchange (ALE)	.ale
Quantel Harry	.vtr
Flex	.flx

Table 7.2   ALE Export Formats

Film and Matchback options are not available on all Avids, so it must be determined if any of these are supported on the system. The easiest way to do this is to launch the application.When the project selection screen appears, create a new project. If the film options are available on the system, they'll appear at the bottom of the new project screen. There are two types of film options available. The first, Film Options is used when a 24 fps project is desired. The second, Matchback Options, is used if the editor wants to work in 30 fps but match the **EDL** back to original film numbers. If any of these options is grayed out on the project screen, that option isn't available for that particular Avid. if none of the options is selected, the application will assume that the project is a video project and will not be able to create a cut list. Entering key numbers and ink numbers will be impossible. This may seem obvious, but many editors ignore this in haste. Film and matchback options come in three gauges: 16mm, 35mm, and 65mm. After choosing between 24 fps or Matchback, choose the film gauge and open the project.

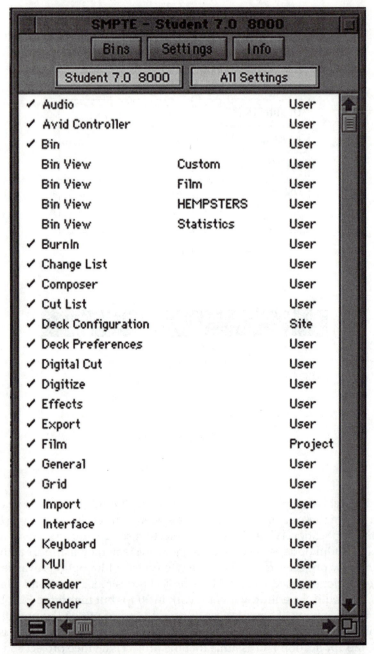

Figure 7.2   Avid Project Window: Note Settings files are alphabetical

Table 7.3 Avid Film Settings

Film Setting	Menu Item	Description
Sequence time code Format	Video (30 fps)	Time code of the finished edit is measured at 30fps (Default)
	Film (24fps)	Time code of the finished edit is measured at 24fps
Ink Number Format	35mm 16 fr/num	Standard for both Key and Ink, numbered every foot of film.
	16mm 20 fr/num	Most common standard for Key numbers. Every 1/2 foot of film
	16mm 40 fr/num	Some film manufacturers have 16mm key numbers every foot. Also used in some ink number situations.
Ink Number Displayed As	Key code	The system displays key numbers above the monitors on the EC track
	Edge Code (4 Counting)	The system displays Ink numbers with a 4 digit count on the EC track
	Edge Code (5 Counting)	The system displays ink numbers with a 5 digit count on the EC track
Auxiliary Ink Format	35mm,16mm 20fr/num and 16mm 40 fr/num (Same as Ink Number Format Above)	Determines how auxiliary ink numbers will be measured according to the same specifications as Ink Number Format above. Auxiliary Ink numbers are used if the print was inked on two separate occasions.
Auxiliary Ink Displayed As	Key code, Edgecode (4 counting) or Edgecode (5 counting) Same as Ink Number Displayed As (above)	Same descriptions as Ink Number Displayed As above.

Table 7.3 Avid Film Settings (continued)

Film Setting	Menu Item	Description
DAT time code Format	SMPTE 30 fps	For Audio Only in a 24 fps project. DAT time code should be referenced to a true 30 fps.
	SMPTE 29.97 fps	Used only if DAT time code was incorrectly referenced at 29.97 fps during recording.

ADJUSTING FILM SETTINGS

Now that the project is created, it is necessary to tell the Avid how to gauge the film numbers and time code. The film settings are accessed through the setting files in the project window. Film settings are only necessary on 24 fps projects. If a matchback project is created, these settings are not accessible.

Double click on the Film settings in the project window. The Film Settings menu contains several pulldown items that need to be resolved. Avid's nomenclature for edge numbering can be a little confusing. For example, the menu item Ink Number Displayed As refers to both key numbers and ink numbers. Ink numbers are also referred to as edge code, which normally could refer to either ink or key numbers.

IMPORTING ALE FILES

To import ALE files into an Avid project, it is first necessary to create a bin in which to store them. I highly recommend creation of a bin for each cam roll. From this bin, scene bins can be created, one for each scene in the film, and clips can be copied for each scene to those bins from the original cam roll bins by option-dragging them over.

This organizational idea isn't new, but it is very efficient. By creating and archiving cam roll bins, the original information remains intact. When the clips within the cam roll bins are copied to specific scene bins, a workspace is created where effects, imported picture files, and scenes can be combined for editing.

Once the cam roll bin is created (by selecting New Bin in the project window), select Import from the File menu. The import screen allows users to import everything from graphics to information. In this case, shot log should be selected. When Shot Log is selected, three options appear on the right of the screen.

Combine events based on scene number and automatically create subclips
Combine events based on the camera roll and automatically create subclips
Merge events with known sources and automatically create subclips

These three items create a powerful array of viewing and subclipping options and allow scenes and clips to be divided in the manner that best fits the editor's and director's style.

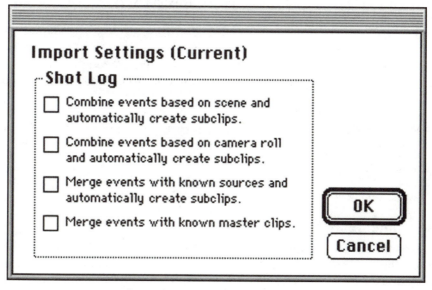

Figure 7.3   Import Shot Log Options

Combining Events Based on Scene Number

Combine events based on scene number makes one large clip of all of the elements within a scene in the log, and then creates subclips of each individual clip recorded in telecine. In order to use this option, the telecine log must contain scene and take information.

Combining Events Based on Camera Roll

Combine events based on the camera roll will produce a large clip for each camera roll and divide individual takes into subclips.

Merging Events with Known Sources

Merge events with known sources creates subclips from a log with sources already inside of the bin. For example, if an entire cam roll is already logged in the bin as one clip, this will take the individual events recorded in telecine and create subclips for that cam roll.

CHECKING KEY NUMBERS

After importing the telecine logs into bins, the material can be batch digitized on the Avid, just like a regular video project. Once the batch digitizing is done, check the key numbers to make sure that everything was recorded correctly. When working in a 24 fps project, digitizing on the fly won't work. All materials must be logged or imported from telecine logs prior to digitization. This is to prevent pull-down errors.

In the time code menu above the source monitor, select EC. This displays the edge code instead of time code. Load each clip and scroll through it, making sure that the EC in the display matches the key numbers burned into the video source. There are a few things in particular that should be detected.

A one-frame delay, which occasionally occurs in telecine.
A frame miscount, which occurs when the film gauge doesn't match the telecine log file.
A completely different set of key numbers, usually caused by incorrectly labeling reels or having two reels with the same name.

One Frame Delays

Occasionally telecine burn-ins encounter a one-frame delay, where the number burned onto the screen is one frame behind the actual key number recorded into the telecine database. Most telecine houses don't have this problem, but it can occur. It originates because the burn-in is created by a key number and time code reader/character generator. During transfer, running the video signal through the reader/generator and then to a VTR can delay the image, thus the burn-in is off by a single frame. If this occurs, the videotape can be sent back with a request for an accurate burn-in or the neg cutter can be notified that the burn-in is behind a frame. Most neg cutters have heard this story before, and though they don't like the inaccuracies, they can deal with it. As long as the database is accurate, there shouldn't have any problems.

But films by nature have problems, and the more that are created, the more difficult it is to keep track of them all. A retransfer is far more desirable and it eliminates concerns over the memory of all of the human beings who will be interacting with the film. If a retransfer is made, be sure to remove all of the "bad" clips and their associated media files from the NLE. Also rename the retransfer reel. For example, reel 001 becomes reel 001R. I use this convention because, though there may be 001B and 001C reels, chances are very unlikely that the reel count extends to R. R is strictly used for retransfer. Ask the telecine logger to rename the new videotape to this in the database as well, which should save a lot of remodification time. Be sure to mark the original transferred reel as "DO NOT USE". I recommend a red thick permanent marker for this purpose, writing on several locations on the tape box and on the labeled tape itself.

Frame Miscounts

Frame miscounts are not as common as one frame delays, but they do happen. Miscounts are usually caused by either an error in telecine databasing or an error in setting up the project on the Avid. I have encountered other odd situations where data was logged incorrectly, but those occurrences are extremely rare.

If it is noticed that the database numbers in the EC display and the burn-in numbers gradually become mismatched, stop everything. Any editing will become worthless. There is a serious problem.

Usually, frame miscounts can be detected right away. The easiest way to troubleshoot a miscount is by looking at the EC display. The EC display is accessible through one of the two time code registers above both the source and record monitors. One of the best features of an Avid is its ability to show the current numbers through the EC display. This allows any frame to be checked at any time for consistency in the numbers. The key number count in the EC display ends with either a "+" or "&" followed by two numbers. If it has a "+," the database assumes that the film is 35mm. If it has a "&," it assumes that it is 16mm. This is a standard for gauging film, although not every NLE application adheres to it.

Figure 7.4   The EC displayed above the sequence monitor on an Avid.

For example, let's say that the film is 16mm but the EC column displays key numbers with a "+". In this instance, the header information in the telecine log may have erroneously been set up as a 35mm project, but the key numbers on the burn-in could be correct. The telecine log could be opened, the information could be changed in the header from 35mm to 16mm and the log could be reimported. The numbers should match. Be sure to destroy the incorrect media files and bins. This problem can be detected when importing the log. A message stating that the log format does not fit the project type will occur. This is the first sign of trouble.

The problem can also be detected by inspecting numbers both in the EC column and burn-in. 35mm film does not count key numbers beyond "+15". If 16, 17, 18, or 19 appears in the EC, the project is set up for 16mm.

Mislabeled or Duplicate Numbered Tapes

One last problem that might occur with checking key numbers is when two separate reels are given the same number. This can occur for a variety of reasons which are too numerous to discuss here. Simply put, if the key numbers in the database or those displayed in the EC column don't look even remotely like the numbers on the screen, chances are that the wrong reel was digitized with the wrong database. This problem occurs frequently, particularly with films that have high shooting ratios. In this case, one could renumber one of the errant reels and modify its name in the database.

USING AUTOSYNC

After the log is imported and digitized, key numbers are checked and the project is organized appropriately, sound and picture can be synched together. If the sound was already transferred in sync with picture at telecine, this step is unnecessary.

Avid's syncing mechanism is called **Autosync** and it works very simply. First, select a picture clip and find the slate. Mark in where the clap boards meet. Then, select the corresponding audio clip. Scrub through the beginning until the frame where you hear the clapper impact is located. Mark in on that frame.

In the bin, select the picture clip, then shift-select the sound clip. Under the Bin menu, select Autosync. A menu appears on the screen. Dailies can be synched by in point, out point, source time code or auxiliary time code. Choose In points and select OK.

A new subclip will appear in the bin, with the extension ".sync.01." Load this clip into the source monitor and play it back. One of the best ways to check that it's synced correctly is to scrub through the slate at the beginning and make sure that the clap sound is in the right place. If the new clip isn't quite right, delete it and re-mark the sound and picture elements until the correct combination is made. In time, you'll gain confidence and will be able to do this very quickly.

There is one limitation to Autosync; the synced subclip ends where the picture stops. If the film is a documentary and the camera stopped but sound continued to roll, it is necessary to add sound separately to the sequence without using the synced clip.

FILM EFFECTS

In addition to Avid's regular effect palette, there are a variety of effects that can aid filmmakers, including mattes, blow-ups, film dissolves and film fades.

Film Dissolves

Film dissolves are not the same as a standard video dissolve. The two sources, which are dissolved "from" and "to" have intensities that are calculated differently during the effect. The result is that if a standard video dissolve on an NLE is used, it looks or "feels" different when an optical print is made on film. During the course of a video dissolve, the intensity of the "from" source declines at the same rate as the "to" source increases. Thus, halfway through this type of dissolve, each source is at 50 percent intensity. That rate remains consistent as "from" becomes more transparent and "to" becomes less transparent.

But an optical dissolve is different. The "from" source remains at full intensity until it is halfway through the effect. The "to" source increases to full intensity at the halfway point. Thus, halfway through the effect, both are at full intensity. During the second half of the effect, the "from" source decreases in intensity until it has disappeared. The "to" source remains at full intensity. So for the second half of the effect, the only thing that is happening is that the "from" source vanishes from the screen.

Depending on the two elements used, the resulting differences between a video and a film dissolve could appear as subtle or completely different, but use of the Avid film dissolve effect is a far more accurate rendition of how the effect will look when screened on film.

Figure 7.5 Optical dissolve (left) and video dissolve (right)

In like manner, a film fade effect combines black or darkness with the picture element at full intensity halfway through the effect. For the second half of the effect, the picture slowly vanishes. Again, it might be a matter of minor nuance, but it is truer to what you'll see when screening the effect on film.

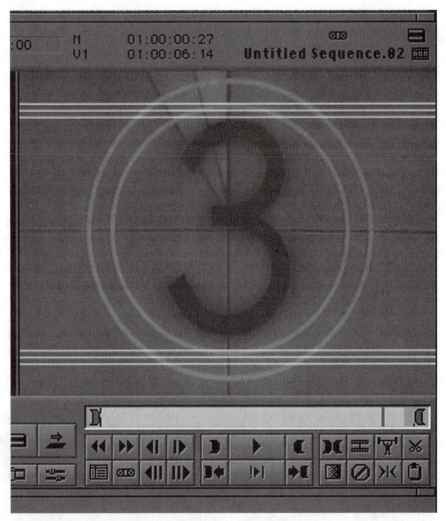

Figure 7.6   Matte outlines via the Grid Tool

Mattes

If the film was shot full frame with the intention of adding a matte, Avid's film mattes are a great tool. The mattes vary in format and are located in the Effects Palette. The following mattes are supported:

16:9
1:1.66 (European Standard)
1:1.85 (American Standard)
1:2.35 (Anamorphic / Super)

The mattes work just like any other Avid effect. Drag one from the Effect Palette and drop it to its intended location. If the matte is to be applied to an entire sequence, create a new video track and drag the effect to the top track. Any real-time effects underneath the matte will need to be rendered in the sequence.

There is also a way to view what a matte will look like before it is applied. Above the sequence monitor is a Fast Menu. Click on the menu and choose Grid. The title safe and action safe borders will appear on the screen in the form of bright white lines. In the Project Settings window, open the Grid settings. Set the grid to show film aspect ratios, and they will appear superimposed over the sequence as white lines. These lines signify the matte sizes. Although they can be seen in the sequence monitor, they do not show up on the NTSC monitor and will not appear in the output.

Blow-ups

Although many NLEs have resizing options and effects, the most accurate one to use in the case of film is a **blow-up**. The reason for this is that a blow-up is not just an effect, it is also a method of conveying information to the optical house that will do the blow-up. For example, if the intention is to increase the screen size by 200 percent and pan the picture slightly left, a blow-up effect can convey the proper information to the opticals house in an optical list. Instead of percentages, the optical house uses fields to define expansion. Instead of left, right, up, and down, they use west, east, north, and south to define orientation of the frame. So if the size or orientation of a frame is changed, blow-up is the best effect to use.

SCRIPT INTEGRATION

Before I get to the business of creating cut lists, I should mention one of the more brilliant options available on Avid NLEs known as Script Integration. Script Integration allows the editor to import a script into the NLE and use it much like the standard lined script that editors are used to using to diagram the coverage on a given scene. The script is treated much like a regular bin, but the editor has the ability to mark it with straight or squiggly lines to indicate dialog and coverage in the same way as a lined script and can record information about the relationship between dialog and the actual clip.

To begin, a script is required. It can be in a text file, but a rich text format (RTF) is better. A rich text format looks pretty much like any script would on paper. When the script is imported and opened in the script bin, it appears in the bin monitor like a word processing document as shown in Figure 7.7. Usually the production office has the script in a word processor format, so it's fairly easy to obtain. To open the script, select Open Script under the File menu. Then double click on the script name in the bin menu.

Note that there are several tools unobtrusively placed above the script. There is a straight line (to indicate dialog spoken on camera), a squiggly line (to indicate dialog spoken off camera), a record button, and play button.

When a scene in the script is located, the corresponding scene bin with clips in it can be opened. Drag the clips and place them appropriately before dialog or the scene description in the script. When the clip is placed in the script, a color thumbnail image of the scene appears with the clip name on it. If there is more than one take of the same shot, drag it on top the original. The end result will be a single thumbnail from the first clip, but the numbers will change below the thumbnail, indicating more than one take. When one of the take numbers is double clicked, that take is loaded into the source monitor. The scene can be played back with coverage or even line-to-line correspondence between the clip and the script recorded.

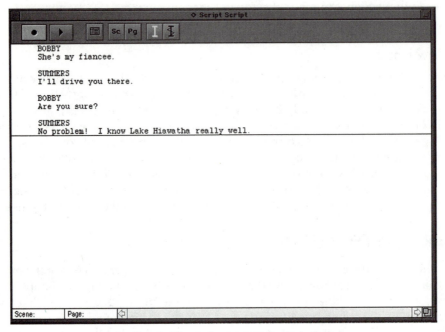

Figure 7.7 The Script Integration Interface

To record script line correspondence, select a take by double clicking its number, then click on the record button in the script monitor. As the take plays back, click on each line of script as the actor delivers it. When the scene is finished playing, click the stop button. The result is that when any line in the script is clicked, the clip cues to that point. This is really helpful when looking for a best performance or delivery of a line. It enables the editor to click on the takes, then the line, and play them back to back, which is difficult to do with a standard NLE bin.

It is also possible to choose between a straight or squiggly line to mark the script to indicate whether the dialog appears on or off camera. Just like a printed lined script, coverage can be determined at a glance without the need to open or play any clips.

USING FILMSCRIBE

Once the cut is completed on the Avid, it's time to create a cut list. As described in Chapter 5, there are many types of cut list. To begin, from the Output Menu, select FilmScribe.

FilmScribe™ is integrated with Avid editing software but is a separate application that can be launched with or without the Media Composer or Xpress running. If FilmScribe is launched while the editing application is running, plenty of memory is needed. 256 MB is a good minimum. Most v.10 Avids come equipped with 384 MB.

If the Media Composer is pre version 8.0 or pre Xpress 3.0, FilmScribe probably isn't available. In this case, Cut List can be used. Cut List is located under the Output menu. The Cut List tool is very similar to FilmScribe, but not as robust. FilmScribe adds a little versatility and a lot of templates to the tool that make it easier to configure and create cut lists. There was also a significant change from Media Composer 5.x to 6.x with the Cut List Tool. For these examples, FilmScribe is used, but the same results can be achieved with any Avid Cut List tool. If some of the options mentioned in this chapter are missing from the Cut List tool, it's probably an earlier version.

After launching FilmScribe, bins can be opened directly from the File menu. In earlier versions of the Cut List tool, this is done by dragging the sequence directly from a bin in the Media Composer or Xpress, which must stay open in order for the cut list tool to work.Because FilmScribe can work as a standalone or modular application, it can be launched separately with the bins opened from FilmScribe or launched from within the Media Composer/Xpress application, where sequences can be dragged directly from the bins into the tool.

Once the sequence bin is opened, bring up the cut list tool. From the File Menu, select New Cut List. After dragging the sequence into the Sequences window of the cut list tool, select the video track where the cut exists. If a matte has been added on a higher track, don't use it. This will only make the list confusing. Every edit should be on a single track in order to maintain a uniform cut list. Normally, a cut list for audio wouldn't be created unless ink numbers are used. In a later section, we'll discuss various methods of audio export.

On the bottom right underneath the Sequences panel is a menu of the various types of list that can be generated with the tool. Global, when selected, opens a list of global options used when generating any of the lists (see Table 7.4). To output each type of list, click on the box located to the left of the list name. To choose options for that particular list, double click on the name.

There are numerous types of lists that can be generated in the tool. These include

Assemble
Optical
Dupe
Pull
Optical pull

Scene assemble
Scene pull
Optical scene pull

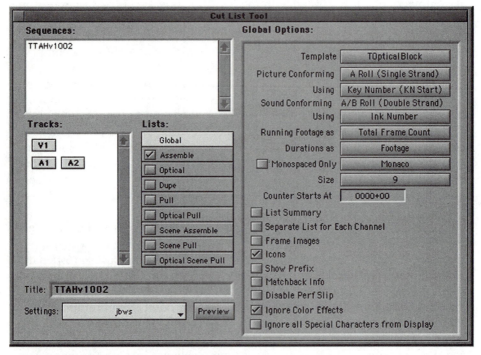

Figure 7.8 The FilmScribe Cut List Tool

Unique Items for Individual Types of Cut Lists

Each list type has several individual options. The individual options for these lists determine which items will be displayed in the final output. Depending on the project, some are important and some are not. For example, if key numbers are used as a source of reference for the film, ink numbers and auxiliary ink wouldn't normally be necessary in the list. Any options that do not have corresponding information in the bins will not have any information in the list. In addition to the common options shared by other lists in Table 7.5, the individual types of cut list have the options shown in Table 7.6, Table 7.7, Table 7.8, and Table 7.9.

Change Lists

In addition to standard cut lists, FilmScribe allows users to create a **change list**. A change list relates to an original cut and a revised cut. It compares the two lists and outputs only change-specific information. This makes the list easier to conform because the person conforming doesn't have to search two entire lists to make a few changes. Change lists work on 24 fps projects only. FilmScribe will generate change lists, change pull lists, and change discard lists. A change pull list determines the clips necessary to pull for creation of the changes. A discard list does the opposite.

Table 7.4   Global Cut List Options

Option Name	Description
Template	TAnimation- a list customized for animation including a running counter, duration, frames and clip names. TColumnar- a simple method of displaying the list in columns that are easy to read. TLog Exchange- Creates the cut list in an ALE format that can be converted back to a Flex file. Flex files are commonly used by some neg cutters. TOptical Block- This is a display of opticals that is more graphical and less textual than the columnar format. Tstoryboard- Displays clip names, scene and take.
Picture Conforming	Selects which format will be used to conform the picture. This mostly affects how dissolves and fades are treated. A Roll (Single Strand) Conforming treats all transition effects as opticals A/B (Double Strand) Conforming places standard length dissolves and fades in the assemble list. These can be done at the lab without creating an optical, so long as their lengths are 16, 24, 32, 48, 64 or 96 frames.
Using	Choose the frame numbering system that is being used for the conform. Usually, it's Key Numbers, but Ink Numbers, Auxiliary Ink Numbers or Film Time code can also be used.
Sound Conforming	For creating sound cut lists, choose between Ink Numbers or Auxiliary Ink Numbers.

Table 7.4 Global Cut List Options (continued)

Option Name	Description
Running Footage As	This option shows feet and frames based upon gauge or a total frame duration. The choices are 16 mm- 40 frames per foot (Standard) 16mm – 20 frames per foot 35mm- 2 perf 35mm- 3 perf 35mm- 4 perf (Standard) 35mm- 8 perf 65mm- 5 perf 65mm- 8 perf 65mm- 10 perf 65mm- 15 perf Total Frame Count
Durations As	Determines durations as footage or frames in the list.
Font	Choose from any fonts on the system, but be aware that some don't line up in the columns as well as others when the list is created. Courier is the default and it tends to line up quite well. Most monospaced sans serif fonts offer the best solution. Try not to get too fancy here. The list needs to be easily readable.
Font Size	Again, simplicity is the key. Make sure that the font is large enough to be easily read but small enough so that the list doesn't run off of the right side of the page when printed.
Counter Starts At	Determines the footage count where the cut list begins. Default would be 00000+00.
Summary List	When this checkbox is selected, a summary of all of the cut lists is generated.
Separate Lists for Each Channel	This option, when selected, generates different lists for each channel of video selected in the Cut List Tool. Be careful. If it's necessary to make a cut list from several tracks, it will ignore any multi track effects and only generate information about the foreground of the effect. Multi-track lists are generally not used. The picture track, where elements were combined and picture was cut, should be the cut list track. Normally the cut list will combine elements from multiple tracks unless this option is selected.

Table 7.4 Global Cut List Options (continued)

Option Name	Description
Matchback Info	This option displays what modifications were necessary when creating a 24fps list from a 30 fps matchback. For example "Matchback trimmed −1 frame" underneath a cut that had to be trimmed for time.
Disable Perf Slip	Not available in matchback. A perf slip in a 24fps project allows the editor to slip sound in perforations, not frames to more closely match sync.
Frame Images	Displays a thumbnail image in the list for each starting frame of each cut.
Icons	Allows inclusion of representative icons in A/B conformed assemble lists only for dissolves, fades, dupes, jump cuts and freeze frames. Only standard duration fades and dissolves are included. All others go to the optical list.
Show prefix	Shows entire key number, including its generic prefix, at both start and end numbers in the list. Deselect this item to show the prefix only on the start number and therefore save some printing space on the list.
Ignore Color Effects	Ignores information about color effects in the cut list.
Ignore Special Characters	Generates the cut list without graphic icons, Quicktime™ movie images or header images.

All of the global options previously mentioned apply as well to change lists. Common options are identical as well. Table 7.10 shows a list of specific options available on change lists.

Preview Code

If you've conformed a workprint and are going through the process of making some changes, it is wise to create **preview code** on the previously conformed print. Preview code consists of ink numbers that are placed on the workprint before changes are made. Preview code information can be included in a change list to simplify the process of making changes to the workprint. If ink numbers were used to complete the original conform, preview code can be generated in another ink color directly on the cut workprint to distinguish between the two.

Table 7.5 Common Cut List Options

Option Name	Description
Key Numbers	Reference numbers based upon KN Start and KN End in the bins.
Ink Numbers Aux. Ink Numbers Lab Roll Camera Roll Sound Roll Reel Slate Comments Scene & Take Locators	All of these items can be listed, but are dependent upon whether or not each was noted in the bins. Locator and comment information in the sequence, such as special music or sound effects cues, color correction, or other important data, can also be included. Of special import to the neg cutter are Camera Roll and Scene & Take.
Clip Name	This places the designated name for the clip in the cut list. Normally, this isn't necessary if Scene & Take are included, as the clip name in a film is normally the same.
Custom Column from Bin	This option allows placement of information from a customized column into a bin. For example, if a custom column were created that contained sound notes, it could be included in the list. Be careful not to go overboard with this item, as the list will end up overrunning the printed page. If this item is chosen, be sure to use the same spelling and case that was used for the original name in the bin.
Record TC	This places the time code from the master sequence into the list. It is especially helpful if a videotape digital cut of the sequence is included with the list so that the neg cutter can cross reference it.
Address TC Film TC Sound TC Aux TC 1-Aux TC 5 24 TC 25p TC 25 TC 30 TC	These are other time code types that can be used when digitizing that might be necessary for generating a cut list. For example, if time code from a sound source was generated on audio track 2 and then read by the Avid, it would normally be input as an auxiliary TC. If a list is needed for this source, the cut list can generate it. If Film Time Code was used, it could be used as an alternative source for cutting the film rather than using Key Numbers.

Table 7.6 Unique Assemble List Options

Option Name	Description
LFOA	Last Frame of Action. Determines duration of a reel at the LFOA. You can subtract footage at the head or tail of the reel to determine the proper duration. Head would normally be on the picture start frame, tail would be after the LFOA.
Mark Short Cuts Shorter Than	If this item is checked, the list will flag cuts shorter than a specified number of frames with a comment. This can be helpful to the person conforming.
Mark Jump Cuts Shorter Than	In this case, a jump cut is defined as where a short piece of material is missing between adjacent cuts of the same material. When selected, the list will flag jump cuts shorter than a specified number of frames with a comment.
Show Trans Effects As Cuts	This item is especially useful for conforming workprint, so that instead of leaving blank space for an optical, the list will tell where the optical goes so that it can marked with a grease pencil or tape.

Table 7.7 Unique Optical List Options

Option Name	Description
Key Frames	This determines whether the optical keyframes are taken from the composition itself. If any changes might be made to the optical keyframes of an effect, it's a good idea to choose this option.
Optical Footage	Shows footage relative to the beginning of an optical
Page Break Between Opticals	Creates a separate page for each optical in the list.

Table 7.8 Unique Dupe List Options

Option Name	Description
Tolerance/Assume Handles	Tolerance sets the size of handles during dupe checking, but calculates the handles to each side of the clip internally, rather than putting the handles into the list
Print w/ Handles	This sets the size of handles after checking for dupes in the list. The given number of frames selected with this option is added to the beginning and end of each clip in the list.

Table 7.9 Unique Pull and Scene Assemble List Options

Option Name	Description
First Sort By Then Sort By Then Sort By	Establishes a hierarchy of how the list is to be configured, a pecking order of which criteria is most important in how it is displayed. It can be sorted by the following criteria: Lab Roll Camera Roll Sound Roll Scene & Take Clip Name

After the first order of sorting is selected, there is also the option of "none" for the second and third order of sorting. For example, if you only wanted the list sorted by Camera Roll, select it as the First Sort By item and then select None in the other two items. |
| Sort Order | Choose how the clips will be sorted, either heads out (ascending edge numbers) or tails out (descending edge numbers) This is dependent upon how the person conforming, either neg cutter or assistant editor, stores the rolls. |

Table 7.9   Unique Pull and Scene Assemble List options

Option Name	Description
Place Separators	Creates a horizontal separator in the list, which can make it easier to access specific information at a glance. Choose where the separator is placed from the following options: First Sort Field Second Sort Field Key code or Ink Prefix Prefix or every 1000 feet (no separators)
Include Opticals Include Headers	Specifies whether or not opticals and headers are to be included in the list.

Table 7.10   Change List Options

Option Name	Description
Show Only Changes	Selecting this option shows only insertions, deletions, trims and moved clips. When deselected, the list will elicit details about unchanged sections as well.
Combine Deletions	Allows groups of adjacent deletions to be included in one event. However, selecting this option disables generation of discard lists, which specifically list each deletion as a separate event.
Preview Code	Displays preview code numbering. (See below details)
Counter Starts At	Determines the footage count where the change list begins. Default would be 00000+00.

Quicktime Options

One of the features of FilmScribe is its ability to show Quicktime movies of the sequence from within the list. This works handily for verification. In order to show the Quicktime movies, they'll need to be exported from the Avid. It's something of a time consuming process. Still, if FilmScribe is used as a standalone application, it works well and allows viewing of burn-in numbers as the list is browsed.

EXPORTING AUDIO

Audio can be exported from the project by digital cut, OMF file conversion or EDL.

Digital Cut

If the audio is exported via digital cut to tape, keep in mind that somewhere along the line, the audio will have to be conformed to its proper speed. If the audio is exported directly to tape from a matchback project and played at speed with a cut film, it wouldn't work. The audio has to be resolved at +.01 percent faster. For further details on sound sync issues, see Chapter 4.

OMF

Audio media and sequences can be exported through the use of OMF, also called **OMFI**, or Open Media Framework Interchange. OMFI is ambitious; it is a common format allowing media to be shared not only cross-application but also cross-platform. OMFI is supported on most digital audio workstations and is frequently used for exporting audio media files between computers. Conversion to a proper format requires the OMF tool, which is available on most workstations and also is downloadable through Avid and Digidesign's websites. OMF will export cuts, dissolves, level information, time code, track numbers and clip names. It does not export pan information or automation gain.

OMF files consist of two items: compositions, which are the framework of the edited sequence, and media. The OMF composition can be exported by itself if the media is already on a workstation. Most OMF compositions and media files from feature-length films can be exported onto high capacity removable format drives, including Iomega Jaz or Castlewood Orbs. For short films, Zips might be used, but, depending on the complexity of the audio tracks, they might not fit.

Before exporting the audio into OMF, some preparations must be made. First, make a copy of the master sequence and place it in a separate new bin. Load the duplicate sequence in the record monitor and delete any video tracks. This can be done by clicking on the video track selectors and pressing the delete button on the keyboard. The system will verify that this is being done intentionally. Click on Yes. Render any audio effects, including dissolves, mix downs, etc. before exporting.

The next step is to consolidate the media to a drive. It can be a removable media or an empty drive that can be moved to the sound department. In any case, I highly recommend that the drive be completely empty, to allow the necessary space. There is nothing worse than the near completion of consolidation that is interrupted by a "not enough room on this drive" message. The Avid does not precompute the amount of space necessary to make the consolidation ahead of time, so good planning is the best solution.

In its bin, click on the duplicate sequence. From the Clip menu, choose Consolidate. When the Consolidate menu appears, deselect the first two items. Select the proper disk where the consolidated media will be placed. Be sure to give each clip some handles so that the sound department can adjust the audio as necessary. Click OK. It takes a while to consolidate, so be patient.

The OMF Export

With the consolidated audio-only sequence highlighted in the bin, click on the File menu and choose Export. When the export menu appears, choose OMFI Audio and Composition.

If specifically exporting to a Pro Tools system, choose OMFI Composition Only and check the SD2 Format Audio items. This will allow a simpler export to Pro Tools. The audio can then be converted from OMF to Pro Tools/SD2 using the OMF Tool.

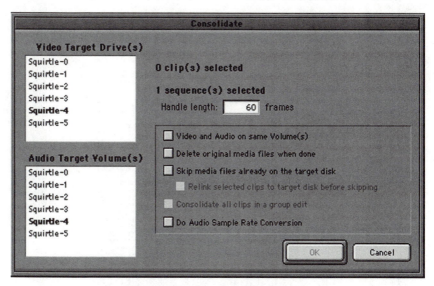

Figure 7.9 The Consolidate menu

If Media Composer version 6 or lower is used, there is a choice of OMFI versions. Most systems use OMFI 2.0, but it is wise to check with the sound department ahead of time to see which they will require.

Click the OK button on the Export menu and the audio exports to the drive.

Exporting an EDL

An EDL, or edit decision list, tells the tale of every cut made in a sequence. For films, EDLs are commonly used for audio. EDLs contain information about the audio, including source and record time codes, but unlike OMFI, they cannot contain media. EDLs are an excellent way of exporting sound information to workstations that do not use OMFI. They are also a good reference source for audio spotting sessions and mixes.

To export an Avid EDL, use EDL Manager, Avid's EDL generating standalone application. This application is bundled on most Avid systems. It also works in tandem with Media Composer and Xpress, so it can be launched through the Output menu in those applications. Warning: Before launching EDL Manager from Media Composer or Xpress, make sure the system has enough memory to do it. Some systems have too little memory for both applications to run at the same time, particularly if the sequence is long and complicated.

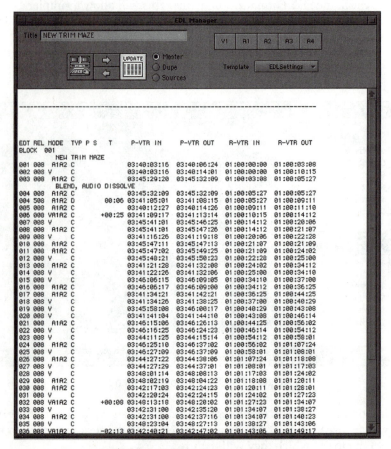

Figure 7.10   EDL Manager Screen

To begin the EDL export, launch EDL Manager. The EDL Manager screen appears, shown in Figure 7.10. If EDL Manager was launched from within the Media Composer or Xpress application, click and drag the sequence into the EDL tool. If EDL Manager was launched separately, select Open from the File menu. Select the bin where the sequence is located. A window will open with all of the sequences in the bin listed. Choose the correct sequence and open it.

Select the tracks that are needed to generate the EDL. Below the tracks are Format and Sort Mode. Unless instructed otherwise by the sound department, choose CMX 3600 as the format and A (Record In) as the sort mode. CMX 3600 is the most universally readable format and almost every audio workstation has a method of reading and sorting CMX lists. A Mode sorting lists the sound in the order that it appears in the sequence.

Additional options for the list can be chosen by clicking on the Options button in the EDL Manager. More information can be added to the EDL by selecting items in the Comments column. Select Optimize EDL from the optimization menu and be sure to choose NTSC or PAL in the Standards column.

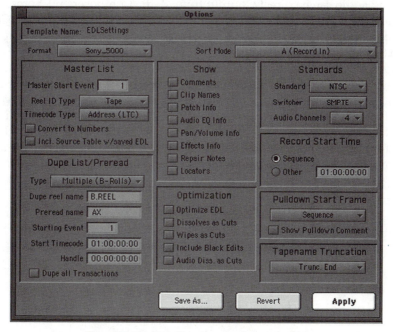

Figure 7.11   EDL Manager Options Window

Saving the EDL

An EDL can be saved to a floppy disk or removable media. If a floppy disk is chosen, format the disk to DOS format. All Apple computers made today are capable of reading DOS formatted disks, so this makes it more universal for audio workstations that read DOS.

From the File Menu, choose Save EDL. Make sure it is saved to the correct disk. The EDL is saved.

Some Important Notes about Saving EDLs

It is better to use eight characters or fewer when naming the EDL. If the name for the EDL is too long, the EDL Manager will truncate it for the proper format and add the proper extension to the name file. Do not change the name after this point, or it might not read properly when imported.

Using EDL Manager, a disk can be formatted specially for Grass Valley Group (**GVG**) or CMX editing systems in **RT-11**, a DOS derivative format. In most cases, this is unnecessary, however, because modern GVG and CMX systems can read DOS.

OUTPUTTING VIDEO

Video and audio can be directly output from Media Composer and Xpress. There is one particular option that is very helpful for conforming; when Digital Cut is selected from the Output menu on a 24 fps project, there are options of outputting at Film Speed (100%) or Video Speed (100+%). If film speed is selected, the output will proceed at the standard frame rate with pulldown for video playback. However, if video speed is selected, the output will proceed with no pulldown and a frame-to-frame correspondence of video to film. Playback of this output would produce sped up sound. The purpose of Video Speed output is to make a lok box for conforming, not for playback. Pulldown fields tend to hinder using videotape for conforming, but with a frame-to-frame correspondence, the person conforming knows that the cut should be frame accurate. This is especially helpful if conforming a workprint is bypassed with the intention of conforming straight to neg.

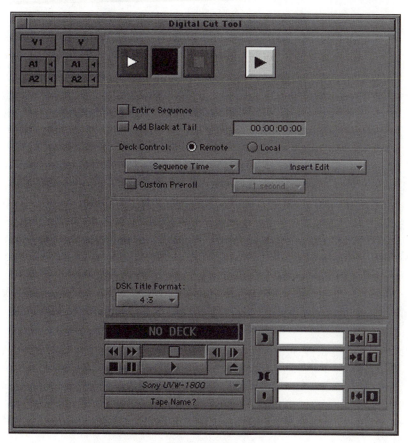

Figure 7.12   Digital Cut Output Options

Chapter 8:
Editing Film on Media 100 NLEs with Slingshot Pro

In this chapter, we'll take a look at integrating film with two popular applications, Media 100 and Trakker Technologies Slingshot Pro.

ABOUT MEDIA 100

Media 100 is a digital 30 fps NLE. It is built for video editing and does not have any special features, effects or listing capabilities that relate to film. Media 100, Inc. recently made a move toward producing NLEs for interactive and web output. They acquired Terran, Inc. and have been focused primarily on furthering the development of streaming video and interactive technology. There are a great many Media 100 systems in the market with several options and features. None of these relate to film. This necessitates the use of a matchback program. In this chapter, we'll look at using the Media 100 with Slingshot Pro.

ABOUT SLINGSHOT AND TRAKKER TECHNOLOGIES

Trakker Technologies' Slingshot Pro is a suite of applications for matching back EDLs from NLEs with the original telecine log. It should be noted that Slingshot Pro is very robust and can work with just about any NLE made, including Avid and Final Cut Pro. Slingshot Pro consists of three stand alone applications:

The Telecine Log Converter (TLC) converts the four most common log types into batch digitize lists for all major NLEs.

The Film Trakker converts video EDLs into 24 fps film cut lists, including assemble, dupe, optical, pull, and optical pull lists.

The Sound Tracer traces information from any telecined audio back to its original time code in the database. If audio is digitized separately, there is not normally a need for this application. However, it is an absolute necessity for finding the original numbers of sound transfers done in telecine.

DRAG AND DROP FUNCTIONALITY

Slingshot's biggest asset is its drag and drop functionality. From the first few pages of the User Guide, it's easy to learn how to set up the applications and drag the proper files in and out for a fast and easy matchback. There are so many options that one could select when using matchbacks that it could be overwhelming. Slingshot sticks to the important items and pretty much ignores fancy window dressing. It's configurable to a number of specifications, but also is easy to run.

In order to do the work, Slingshot creates an intermediary file between the original telecine log and the final EDL. This file, called the Telecine Log Converter file or TLC (not to be confused with Time Logic Control) is the key to creating successful lists.

Slingshot lets the databases do their work without interference. Instead of having to database each shot that has already been databased in the telecine logs, Slingshot translates them into the language of the target NLE rather than making the editor redo work that's already been done.

SUPPORTED TELECINE LOGS

Slingshot's Telecine Log Converter will convert from the four most popular formats of telecine log, which are shown in Table 8.1. Telecine Log Converter will create three types of files from the original telecine logs: they are import logs, TLC files, and dailies logs.

Table 8.1 Telecine Log Converter Input Formats

Log Type	File Name = Tape name + Extension
Keyscope Telecine Logs	.KSL
FLEX Telecine Logs (aka "Flex Files)	.FLX
Evertz Telecine Log	.FTL
Avid Log Exchange	.ALE

Import Logs

Import logs are the files converted by TLC for batch digitizing with the NLE. These files are created specifically for the type of NLE that is being used. Once imported into the NLE, the individual clips in the files can be batch digitized. TLC will output Adobe Premiere, Avid Log Exchange, D-Vision, EMC, Media 100 Power Log, Discreet Edit, Scitex/ImMix, Speed Razor and Final Cut Pro input files. As seen in Figure 8.1, just about any type of NLE is supported.

TLC Files

TLC files contain the vital information necessary for Slingshot to perform film and sound matchbacks. Be sure to keep these in a folder in a safe place. It also isn't a bad idea to copy the TLC files onto a removable form of media for archive. Without these files, a matchback is impossible, so plan wisely. They will be used at the end of the edit to create the final cut lists and sound EDL.

Dailies Log

The dailies log is created for the use of the assistant editor or editor. The dailies log contains vital information in detail for each day of telecine transfer. It also serves as a tool for proofreading log information and correcting any errors in the database. The dailies log will contain key numbers, camera roll, sound roll, sound time code, video time code, reel name, and scene and take entries. The dailies log can be printed and placed in a binder for use in conjunction with camera reports, sound reports, and script supervisor notes.

LOG CONVERSION PROCEDURE

Before starting TLC, create three new folders to hold your TLC, import files and dailies logs. TLC will work with these folders later when the preferences are adjusted. Launch TLC. The pop-up menu shown in Figure 8.1 appears.

TLC Preferences

Before any logs are converted, it's necessary to adjust the preferences to choose a destination folder for each of our TLC file outputs. First, click on the pop-up menu and choose the editing system being used (in this case, Media 100). Next, select the destination folders under Preferences. The screen shown in Figure 8.2 appears.

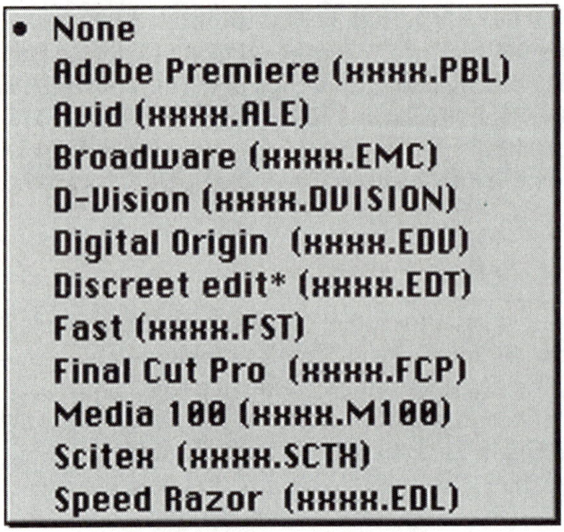

None
Adobe Premiere (xxxx.PBL)
Avid (xxxx.ALE)
Broadware (xxxx.EMC)
D-Vision (xxxx.DVISION)
Digital Origin (xxxx.EDV)
Discreet edit* (xxxx.EDT)
Fast (xxxx.FST)
Final Cut Pro (xxxx.FCP)
Media 100 (xxxx.M100)
Scitex (xxxx.SCTX)
Speed Razor (xxxx.EDL)

Figure 8.1 TLC Pop-Up Menu

In the Preferences menu, destination folders and track enabling can be selected for the conversion. Once this is set, drag and drop telecine logs on the TLC application and it will automatically place the results in the appropriate folders.

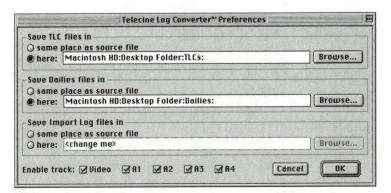

Figure 8.2 TLC Preferences menu

Choosing Destinations

For each TLC, dailies and import log, save the files in the three separate folders created earlier. For purposes of organization, it is recommended to use separate folders. If a single folder is used, the organization of the project becomes muddled and files are harder to find. Choose the destination by clicking on the Browse button and navigating to the proper folder. If Browse is grayed out, deselect the Same Place As Source File option by clicking on the Here radio button.

Enable Tracks

Sometimes telecine databases include audio tracks that need not be digitized. As a result, if the telecine files are directly converted and batch digitized as databased, you'll eat up a lot of drive space on your NLE digitizing redundant or empty sound tracks. This error can be reduced by examining the source tapes and determining which tracks actually contain audio that needs to be digitized. Usually this information is on the label, however, the transfer could also have included redundancy between tracks one and two, in which case, only one track needs digitization.

When the proper tracks are selected under Enable Tracks on the preferences window, it will eliminate unnecessary tracks on the batch digitize Input list for the NLE, thus saving time and drive space. Undoing this in the NLE is time consuming and tedious. Better to do it here before importing.

Syntax Error Correction

Telecine logs can potentially contain incorrect or missing information. This results in redigitizing, clip modification, bogus bins and media files, and other nasty artifacts. When converting logs through TLC, any syntax errors will be flagged before the conversion is complete. The syntax checker in TLC is rather sophisticated, with a WYSIWYG debugging-type screen that not only explains the error, but shows it in the text of the log file.

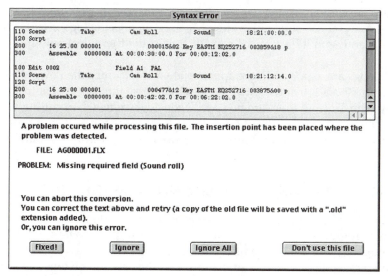

Figure 8.3   Syntax Error screen in Telecine Log Converter

When a syntax error occurs, the top of the screen shows the error in the native file. An insertion point cursor has been placed on the errant section of the text. Below the text is an explanation of why the file was not converted, the file name, and the problem. At the bottom of the screen is an explanation of options and the actions that can be taken. With syntax errors, there are four options from which to select at the bottom of the screen.

Fixed! Choosing Fixed! indicates that the text at the insertion point has been adjusted and the error is fixed. For example, if a scene number is missing, the insertion point is placed next to the Scene entry in the log. Type in the proper number and then choose Fixed! If Fixed! is selected, be careful not to accidentally ruin the formatting of the file by placing spaces in between the entries. If the other entries in the log shift disproportionately, it is possible that another syntax error has been created. In any event, if this error occurs, abort the conversion and start over again.

Ignore. If the error is ignored, TLC will continue with the log conversion. But be warned! Ignoring the error in a telecine log could have disastrous results. The logs could contain inaccurate information or even be incomplete. On some occasions, I've had the misfortune of making this error, only to have the director ask, "Where's take 11?" to which I respond, "I didn't know we had a take 11." Which leads to a mad skimming of the camera reports, which leads to investigating the original logs which leads to total recall of a bumbling error on my part.

Ignore All. Be sure that you feel confident when choosing this option. Ignoring All pretends that any syntax errors don't exist. Although there may be a known consistent error in the log, it could also contain a few surprise errors as well. Choosing Ignore All will bypass any errors encountered. See the previous anecdote for potential results.

Abort. If you feel squeamish about debugging telecine logs, simply choose Abort and send it back to the telecine house. Let them deal with it.

Once the logs are exported in the appropriate format, enter the Power Batch capture tool in Media 100 and digitize as usual. Because the lists are controlled externally by Film Trakker, there are no special considerations when cutting with Media 100 except for creation of lab standard dissolves for A/B conforming, normally used with 16mm films. Film Trakker uses the laboratory standard lengths.

SYNCHING PICTURE WITH SOUND IN MEDIA 100

Synching up in Media 100 is about as easy as it gets. To do this, you'll need to create a new program in the timeline for every clip that needs to be synched. Before you begin, it is wise to create a new bin for synched clips to avoid any confusion with clip names. The original audio and video clips should be together in the same bin.

First, load the video into the timeline. Double click on the video clip to make it appear in the Edit Clip window. Look for the first frame where the clapper contacts the slate. Press Control-F6 (the function key) to mark that point on the clip. A small blue triangle appears at the current time indicator in the timeline. That triangle is the sync mark.

Next, load the audio clip into the timeline so that it overlaps the video, and scrub through it until the first frame of the clapper is heard. Waveforms can also be used to see the sound. From the Track menu, select Show Audio Waveform. It may be necessary to zoom in to the timeline a bit to see the waveform. When the frame where you can first hear (or see, with audio waveforms enabled) the clapper connect is found, press Control-F6 to put a sync marker on that frame of the current time indicator. Holding the option key down, click on the video track and drag it so that the two blue sync markers connect in the timeline. Holding down the option key will cause the two to snap together. Select both the audio and video clips by clicking on the first clip, then shift-clicking on the second clip. From the Program menu, select Sync Clip. The clips in the timeline will turn pink, signifying that the clips are synched together. Click and drag the synchronized clips from the timeline into the new bin.

With each synchronization, it is important to check for accuracy. I find it somewhat common to be off a frame when synching up clips. If you find yourself in this predicament, no problem. Re-mark the originals and do it again, until you get it right.

Some Media 100 users recommend deleting the original video and audio clips- not the media, mind you, but the clips. I highly recommend that you not do this. Instead, place them in an archive bin, where they can be accessed in the event of an emergency.

A project can be organized in a Media 100 in exactly the same fashion that I mentioned previously in the Avid chapter. Import the log and place it in a cam roll bin. Copy the clips and place them in separate scene bins. When you sync up clips, create synched scene bins and use them there. This redundancy allows you to have a backup in case unforeseen bin corruption or sync issues are later discovered.

That's not to say that NLEs regularly lose bin information. In my entire nine years of working with NLEs, I've lost only two bins to corruption. But in both cases, I recovered the information because the clips were redundant in other bins. Most NLEs have a recovery process for missing clip information, but who wants to go through that in the middle of an edit?

Because Media 100 is a video editing machine, audio sync can only be frame accurate, as opposed to perf accurate. Most 35mm film formats have four perfs per frame, so when cutting on a traditional bench, it's easier to attain sync by slipping the audio track a perf or two. Avids have the ability to slip perfs in 24 fps projects. Still, missing sync by a perf or two is common. If you look closely at filmed television, you'll see it all the time.

Media 100 has a full suite of effects, but most don't have a lot to do with filmmaking. An exception is its matting capability, which can allow you to letterbox for appropriate formats. When creating dissolves, be sure to make them center-point dissolves at lab standard frame counts to avoid additional optical costs.

After the film is edited, it's time to output EDLs. For Slingshot, output either CMX 3600 (most commonly used), CMX 3400, or GVG 4.0-7.0 EDL formats.

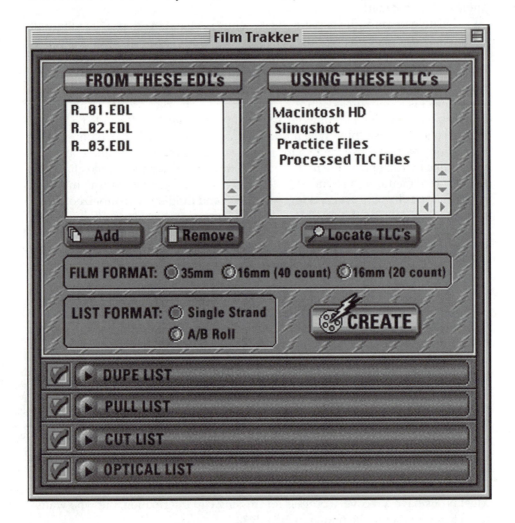

Figure 8.4   Film Trakker Interface

FILM TRAKKER

Once the EDLs are output from the Media 100, use Film Trakker to generate your cut lists. The Film Trakker program works very simply, comparing the TLC file, which contains both key numbers from the film and transfer tape time code to the video EDL. First, launch the Film Trakker application. The FT interface appears, as shown in Figure 8.4.

Film Trakker Preferences

Before creating the lists, be sure to select preferences. Each one of the Preferences must be selected before an accurate list can be generated. Once saved, the preferences will work automatically, as described with TLC.

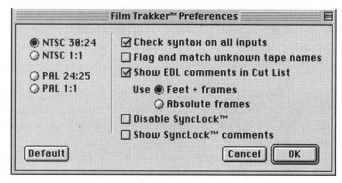

Figure 8.5 Film Trakker Preferences

Table 8.2 Film Trakker Format Preferences

Film Trakker Format Preferences	Description
NTSC 30:24	Use this option if the film was shot at 24 fps, then transferred at 24 fps to video at 30 fps. (29.97fps)
NTSC 1:1	Use this option if the film was shot and transferred at 30 fps to video at 30 fps (29.97 fps)
PAL 25:24	Use this option if the film was shot and transferred at 24 fps to video at 25 fps (PAL B Telecine- See Chapter 3)
PAL 1:1	Use this option if the film was shot at 24 or 25 fps then transferred at 25 fps to video at 25 fps (PAL A Telecine- See Chapter 3)

Format

There are four formats available, as shown in Table 8.2.

Check Syntax on All Inputs

Choosing this option turns on the syntax checker when comparing EDLs to TLC files. The syntax checker with Film Trakker works exactly as it does with TLC.

Flag and Match Unknown Tape Names

As Film Trakker reads the EDLs, it looks for syntax errors and any unknown sources. To ensure accuracy, select this option so that Film Trakker will spot any unknown tapes that exist in the EDL that aren't in the TLC files. There could be a few reasons to use this option.

1. A tape has been digitized into the NLE without transferring its telecine log. Film Trakker will need the right information to correctly produce the cut list. Transfer the telecine log with TLC so that Film Trakker can find the proper corresponding key numbers.
2. The name of an existing tape was changed. In this case, match the new tape name in the EDL to an existing tape number that was previously used to designate the same tape.
3. You've forgotten or missed running a log through TLC. Make sure that all of the logs are converted and saved in the same folder so that Film Trakker can use them.

When Film Trakker encounters a Flag and Match error, there are three options.

Table 8.3   Flag and Match Options

Flag & Match Error Option	Description
No Match	This tells Film Trakker that there is no match, i.e., that a telecine log doesn't exist for this reel.
This One	Selects the reel highlighted on the left side of the screen in the tape list.
Ignore Remaining	Ignore is rarely a good idea when it comes to matching lists, but if you're creating a combined list of film & video, I could see why you might want to avoid the annoyance of flag & match warnings. Just remember, you asked for it.

Disable SyncLock

SyncLock is the process that Film Trakker uses to maintain correct sync between picture and sound, as all matchback programs must do. (See Chapter 6 for details on how matchback works.) If sound sync is not important for your list and the duration poses no problems ("Running Short" and "Running Long" in Chapter 6), then you can disable this option. For most purposes, you'll want to keep SyncLock on.

Show EDL Comments

This option transfers comments from the EDL to their corresponding event in the cut list.

Use Feet + Frames vs. Absolute Frames

This option allows the choice between showing durations in the cut list as feet+frames or absolute frames. Most editors like footage, but animators prefer absolute frame counts, for the most part.

CUT LIST OPTIONS

Film Trakker creates cut lists (also called assemble lists), dupe lists, pull lists and optical lists. The options for each type of list are selected by clicking on the twirl down button on the Film Trakker interface next to the list that is selected (see Figure 8.4). Here are the contents of each list and the configurable options.

Cut List

The cut list for Film Trakker includes the following entries: event number, footage (feet + frames or absolute frames), record time code, duration (for both film and video), first and last key number (a.k.a. key number in and key number out), cam roll number, and clip name (normally the scene and take numbers).

The following options are available on the cut list tool:

Include Optical Count allows for opticals to be included in the assemble cut list. It's convenient to see all of the events in the list. However, this is not recommended for use with the optical house. Most optical houses just want to see opticals, not everything else in the movie. The cut list makes allowances for lab standard dissolves on A/B conforms and includes them in the cut list, not the optical list.

The **start frame** is a footage counter and is expressed in feet and frames, normally starting at 0000+00. Check with the neg cutter before assigning a number. Some start with 0000+00, others prefer every frame counted and start at 0000+01.

Dupe Lists

Film Trakker's dupe lists can be traced across several EDLs. For example, if you build 7 reels for a feature, Film Trakker will check all of the reel EDLs for dupes at a single time. It's a good idea to check for dupes after the first cut from time to time. The sooner it is done, the less possibility that the director will fall in love with the cut and want to use both. Dupes are expensive.

The dupe lists include the following entries:

Set – Each duped section is listed as a set of dupes. In this way, you can determine where they're located and which, if any, to eliminate.

EDL – The name of the originating EDL of the dupe.

Time Code- The location of the dupe on your sequence's master time code.

Event- The event number of each duped item according to the cut list.

Footage- The running footage count in the cut list where the dupe occurs.

Duration- Expressed in feet and frames or absolute frames.

First/Last Key- Key numbers, starting and ending.

Cam Roll

Clip Name – The clip name normally identifies scene and take

Dupe List Options

The dupe lists in Film Trakker offer sort and handles options. Normally one would sort a dupe list by Cam Roll first, then by Key Number. However, the following sort criteria are available to choose from:

Footage- where the clip occurs in the edit.
Record TC- master record time code in point.
Duration – length of the duped clips
First Key- Key number start frame
Last Key – Key number end frame
Camera Roll

The number of frames used for handles in the dupe list can also be adjusted. Contact the neg cutter to see how many frames they will need for each dupe.

Pull List

As described in Chapter 6, pull lists help the person conforming the film to pull the clips necessary for conforming a workprint or negative. A Film Trakker pull list contains

Reel & Event- based upon built reels and the event numbers in the cut (assemble) list.

First/ Last Key

Duration- Feet + frames or absolute frames

Cam Roll

Clip Name- scene and take

Pull List Options

Pull lists can be sorted by the same criteria as specified in the Dupe List Options. Normally, pull lists are sorted by cam roll, then first key numbers. There is also the ability to set handles. As before, check with the neg cutter when setting handles.

Additionally, a choice can be made between creating a cut pull or optical pull list, or both. And you can create a global pull list for a set of EDLs or an individual pull list for each EDL.

Optical List

Optical lists contain specific information that needs to be sent to the optical house to create non-standard fades, dissolves, and other effects. This information includes A and B sides of the optical, key numbers of A and B sides, the optical effect and duration of the effect.

Optical List Options

List Format – Choose between a number of optical list formats. The Trakker format looks much like a cut list and is the easiest to read.

Global List- Same as the option on Pull lists. This will create an optical list from several chosen EDLs.

Individual List- Again, same as the option on Pull lists. This creates an optical list for a single EDL only.

CREATING THE CUT LISTS

Before the lists are created, select a format on the Film Trakker Interface. Choose between 35mm, 16mm (40 Count), and 16mm (20 count). After selecting the film gauge, it's necessary to select a conforming format. Standard is single strand for 35mm, A/B for 16mm. For more details on conforming, see Chapter 4. Add all of the EDLs and TLC files. Select the EDLs in the left window, the TLCs in the right. Once the list types are selected at the bottom of the interface, click on Create. The lists can now be viewed, printed, or saved.

Did you notice that I mentioned not one, but multiple EDLs and TLC files? Film Trakker recognizes that filmmakers will create separate built reels for conforming. As a result, you'll need an EDL for each reel. Film Trakker can search across several reels for dupes. If you ran a separate matchback for each reel without one recognizing the other, this would be impossible.

Figure 8.6   Sound Tracer Interface

THE SOUND TRACER

The sound tracer uses the data from TLC logs and EDLs to trace back to time code of the original sound source (DATs or Nagra recordings) so that an EDL can be created for the sound department. You can always go with your NLE sound or an EDL from the videotapes, but if you use sound from an original source, the Sound

Tracer can help you find the original numbers. Most sound departments want the most pristine recordings available, and that doesn't come from videotape!

Using Sound Tracer is like using any other Trakker application. Once the preferences are set, drag and drop EDLs onto the Sound Tracer icon. From there, double click on it to open the interface. Sound Tracer uses the TLC files and the EDLs to determine correct original sound numbers that are used to create the final EDL. Like Film Trakker, it can input CMX 3400, CMX 3600 or GVG 4.0-7.0 EDLs. It outputs these same types of EDLs. Sound Tracer has the same syntax correction as well as flag and match functions as TLC and Film Trakker. After using Slingshot a few times, it became very clear to me that the creators of the application wanted a hassle-free experience for matching back.

Sound Tracer Preferences

Before generating your EDLs, set the Sound Tracer preferences.

Figure 8.7   Sound Tracer Preferences

Standard— Choose NTSC or PAL

Enforce DOS Naming Conventions—Anyone who has been around computers for a while knows that DOS has some limitations on the number of characters used in file names and extensions. If your sound department uses DOS, you need to select this option.

Create Sound Roll List— This option creates a list of sound rolls used in the EDL so that the sound department can pull them for mixing.

Show Clip Name (Sc/Tk) On Output— Shows the scene number and take in the EDL. Sound mixers usually need this type of information to correlate any spotting notes made by the director.

Check Syntax on all inputs— Same as in Film Trakker.

Flag and Match Unknown Tape Names— Same as in Film Trakker.

After the preferences are set, the TLC files are located, an output format is chosen and the tracks to be included in the list are selected, click on the Trace button and Sound Tracer creates the list.

RUNNING THE LISTS

Now that I've gone through every configuration, here's an example of how Slingshot would run with Media 100 if we had the preferences set and the film edited.

Drag and drop all of the telecine logs onto TLC. The logs are converted in your TLC folder. Drag and drop all of your EDLs into Film Trakker. Set up the project under Preferences by choosing the conversion type. Select the type of cut lists that you wish to generate. Click on Create. It's that easy. Save everything and print as required.

Slingshot Pro can tackle matchback as good or better than any other program on the market. But what if you want to a more integrated matchback application that works inside of your NLE? In the next chapter, we'll take a look at FilmLogic, which uses a combination of databasing, plug-ins and reverse telecine.

Chapter 9:
Editing Film on Final Cut Pro NLEs with FilmLogic

In this chapter, we'll examine the methods for cutting films using two relatively new applications. Apple's Final Cut Pro is a very popular nonlinear editing application that was designed for video editing with Apple's Quicktime digital movie format. FilmLogic, a matchback and 24 fps solution made by Focal Point Software, is compatible with Final Cut Pro, Media 100 and Adobe Premiere. It can be used as a standalone application or as a plug in with Final Cut Pro.

FILMLOGIC

FilmLogic consists of a powerful database manager that can create cut lists in two very different ways. Like Slingshot Pro, FilmLogic can compare between telecine and EDL databases to assemble cut lists. But it also works with certain applications as a plug-in, which will allow output of a cut list from within the NLE application. Currently, FilmLogic offers plug-in support for Premiere, Media 100 and Final Cut Pro. It can also be used as a stand alone application in conjunction with Avid, and EditDV as well as the previously mentioned NLEs.

Normally, a plug-in feature would not make that big of a difference. After all, it is still necessary to import the telecine logs into the database to compare work done with the NLE. But when used with an NLE, plug-ins have the ability to bypass time code information and generate a cut list without the need to generate an EDL.

Version 3 of FilmLogic was the first version of the software to add plug-ins. It also offers something once exclusively reserved for more expensive NLEs: 24 fps editing. 24 fps editing with FilmLogic can be achieved in one of two ways: hardware 24 fps or software 24 fps.

Apple's Final Cut Pro can work with almost any type of video capture card. There are a number of new cards coming onto the market with HD capability as well as true 24 fps capture rates. In order to correctly capture at 24 fps and remove pulldown frames from the telecine video, these cards use SMPTE time code information.

As discussed earlier, it is very important to use nondrop frame time code on the telecine masters and audio tapes. Assuming the standard configuration in which an A frame starts at :00 time code and repeats at :05, a 24 fps card knows where to look to remove the extra pulldown fields. The audio remains intact, without need for any time adjustment, because the quicktime file can change its time base to a true 24 fps without altering the audio.

The key to attaining 24 fps has to do with Quicktime architecture. Quicktime, unlike standard NTSC or PAL video, is not limited by a set framerate or frame duration. As a result, 24 fps capability can be achieved within Quicktime by either eliminating the pulldown during digitization with a 24 fps video capture card or removing pulldown with FilmLogic software through a process called reverse telecine.

The ability to reverse the telecine process is relatively new to FilmLogic as is its plug in capabilities. Reverse telecine uses information in the database and Quicktime's ability to change frame rates and alter time base in order to reduce the framrate to 24 fps and remove pulldown fields.

Although Quicktime allows for a reversal of the process, FilmLogic has to recalculate each frame. In Quicktime, a frame is not always the same size and duration. As a result, FilmLogic has to uniformly adjust or conform the frames and match them to the video rate of 23.976. But there's a problem here: the audio has not been reduced .01 percent to accurately reflect the pulldown. Reverse telecine fixes the problem by adding more time to the frames, increasing the frame rate to a true 24 fps, thus negating any audio mismatches in sync.

Just what is FilmLogic? A database? A Quicktime application? A matchback application? A file conversion program? A logging application? The answer is yes.

IMPORTING THE TELECINE LOG

The FilmLogic suite of functions can be used as a plug-in to Final Cut Pro (FCP), allowing the user to operate from a single application. Final Cut Pro was invented for video editing, not film editing. So in order to open a telecine log, it must first be done using FilmLogic.

FilmLogic accepts the four most commonly used telecine logs; TLC or Flex files (.flx), Aaton files (.atn), Evertz files (.ftl), and Avid Log Exchange files (.ale). To convert the telecine logs with FilmLogic, start the application and create a new database. Import the telecine logs into the database. This database will be used later for matching back to the original film numbers. Remember, FCP doesn't have the capability to store the film numbers, so the logs must be in the database to work. Once the logs have been imported into FilmLogic, they can be exported as a Final Cut Pro batch capture list. From there, the project can be digitized in Final Cut Pro.

Keep in mind as the logs are imported that FilmLogic relies on the scene and take fields in the log as key databasing information. To simplify matters, it's a good idea to retain that information in the names of clips used with Final Cut Pro. For example, Scene 37 Take 1 is normally labeled 37/1 or 37-1.

Logging the Database Manually

FilmLogic comes in two distinct flavors: full-blown and FilmLogic LE, a truncated version. FilmLogic LE is, of course, less expensive, but it doesn't allow manual logging. Instead it assumes the use of telecine logs imported into the database. It also does not use any plug in architecture. As such, it is a matchback only program. The full blown version of FilmLogic will allow manual logging, linking files in the database, and the entry of copious amounts of information about each clip and other preferences. I have only used the full version, so all of my descriptions of functions in this book refer to the use of the full version.

To log clips manually, launch FilmLogic and create a new database. Film-Logic, like most Mac programs, can be launched by double clicking on a database file. If the application icon is double clicked, FilmLogic will ask where the database is located. Because one hasn't been created yet, click Cancel. Under the Database menu, select New Database. The new database menu appears, as shown in Figure 9.1.

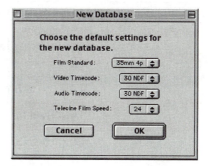

Figure 9.1 New Database Menu

The New Database menu needs some very basic information about the project. There are two important things to keep in mind. First, any mixed formats or gauges are fine with FilmLogic. It can alter frame counts according to gauge independently for each clip. For example, if the project integrates 16mm with 35mm, it could do it. Why would anyone do this? You could never project such a film! I guess the point here is that it can adapt capably and bypass the project settings. Second, if logs are imported, FilmLogic will read the log and bypass project settings for the type or gauge of film specified in the log. This is very important. If the log is incorrect, it will need to be fixed. FilmLogic assumes that the log information is correct (as it should be). So if the project is a 16mm film and the telecine operator forgot to change the gauge type in the database, it will be necessary to alter the log manually with a text editor or reorder the log with corrected information.

Table 9.1 New Database Guide Settings

Setting	Preferences
Film Standard	35mm 4p- 35mm film with four perforations per frame. Standard 35mm gauge.
	35mm 3p- 35mm film with 3 perfs per frame. Used as a film saving device on television shows. Not commonly used on projected film, but easily telecined.
	16mm 20- 16mm film with 20 frames (every 6") between key numbers. Common format, used with Kodak and most other major film manufacturers
	16mm 40- 16mm film with 40 frames (every foot) between key numbers. Less common.
Video time code	30 NDF- 30 fps Nondrop Frame (Actually 29.97) Recommended for film, especially when using hardware reverse telecine to 24 fps.
	30 DF- 30 fps Drop Frame (again, 29.97)
	25 fps- Used for PAL
	24 fps- Used for 24p (see chapter 11)
Audio time code	Same as video preferences.
Telecine Film Speed	24fps- for NTSC pulled down and PAL Telecine B.
	25fps – for PAL Telecine A (25@24fps)

The new database asks for four pieces of information, as shown in Table 9.1. Film-Logic can work with both PAL A and PAL B telecine modes. If PAL A is used, remember that the film will be 4.166 percent faster than normal speed. If audio is digitized separately, it's necessary to adjust it to this speed as well. PAL A projects can be conformed to 24 fps using FilmLogic's conform feature, which will be discussed later in this chapter.

If 24 fps is used as the telecine speed, FilmLogic will create a matchback list because of the variance of framerate. The project can also be digitized on some newer video cards at an accurate 24 fps or use FilmLogic's reverse telecine.

A WORD ABOUT BACKING UP AND UNDO

FilmLogic is a very powerful database, but two things it does not do is back up or undo. As with many databases, once the information is entered, it becomes part of the database record. As a result, it's necessary to make a backup copy from time to time. There is no Save As dialog in FilmLogic, but the project can be backed up by either option dragging the file to a backup folder or dragging it to another drive. It's a good idea to keep previous databases. One never knows when a virus or hardware problem could destroy precious data.

It's important to be aware that once information is entered, there is no Undo function on FilmLogic. Be careful how and when the information is databased.

WORKING WITH FILMLOGIC'S DATABASE

Once the New Database information is defined, two windows will appear on the desktop. These two windows are representations of the database that is being built. One is a list view of found files in the database. The other is detail information about each clip. The **detail view** in FilmLogic is loaded with potential entries of information about each clip. It includes the information shown in Table 9.2. The detail view is the master source of clip information and is filled with both visual and textual information pertaining to each clip. The file is linked to Quicktime files that are used by Final Cut Pro in an editing project. It can also contain a great deal of information that will aid the editor in choosing and organizing shots. Normally, such a robust database would be expected in the NLE, but the creators of FilmLogic chose to go beyond the normal confines of a matchback application and feature some advanced databasing functions.

The **list view** contains a list of records from within the database. The list view can be used to show the results of a search for scene and take criteria or to show the entire database. FilmLogic's programmers claim to be adding more versatility to the Find function in future versions, such as keyword searches.

To list all of the records in the list view, from the Database Menu, select Find (or type Command-F), then select All Records. The list will show all of the records. If all of the records for a specific scene are to be shown, type Command-F and in the scene entry, type the number of the scene and press Return. The found items in the list view will appear.

Table 9.2 Detail View Entries in FilmLogic

Field	Description
Scene Record	Scene Button next to the Scene Identifier field. When pressed, this gives ample space to describe the scene or type in a slug line.
Shot Record	Shot Button next to the Shot Identifier field. When pressed, this gives ample space to describe the shot and scene information.
Scene Identifier	The scene number from the telecine log
Take Identifier	The take number from the telecine log
Cam Roll	Camera Roll
Lab Roll	Lab roll, usually different from the camera roll. Whereas the original camera roll may be 400 feet long, labs often combine the rolls into 2000 ft. rolls
Key code	The key number prefix. Two alphabetic characters followed by six numbers. This field must be typed in correctly or FilmLogic won't accept it.
Film Standard	This is much the same as the film standard established in the project settings, except that it also allows for backward loaded rolls. For example, if the camera assistant loaded a short roll tails out, this feature allows the key numbers to descend and will correctly count key numbers backward in the record and on the cut list.
Key Num	The last four numbers of the key number followed by a frame count, as in 1876+02
Length	Expressed in feet and frames. Frame count uses "&" for 16mm, "+" for 35mm
TK Speed	Normally 24 fps. For PAL projects telecined at 25 fps, 25 fps should be selected.
Vid Reel	The telecine videotape reel number
TC In	Starting time code number
TC Out	Ending time code number
Sound	When clicked, this button allows separate entry of sound time code numbers and sound roll numbers

Table 9.2   Detail View Entries in FilmLogic (continued)

Field	Description
Notes	Additional notes on the shot
Find	Find function currently works to locate Scene and take numbers in the List view. The people at FilmLogic are expanding this feature to be more robust. Future releases will include key word searches.
New	When clicked, creates a new record in the database
Delete	When clicked, deletes a record from the database. Note: there is no undo for this function and no explicit warnings are given prior to deletion.
Save	Saves current record in database.
Previous/ Next Arrows	When pressed moves forward or backward in the List View to details of the previous or next clip.
Open/Find/Choose/ Delete Clip	Normally opens clip. When modified with other keys, this changes function.
Path, Name & Thumbnail	The path name to the corresponding Quicktime file referred to in this record. All records need to be properly linked to their media files to create an accurate cut list.
TK Session	Information about the telecine session is located here.

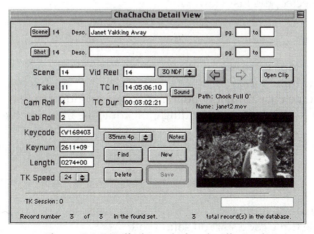

Figure 9.2 Detail View window in FilmLogic

It's important to remember while browsing detailed views in the database that the records shown will only be those in the list view. To browse all files in detail view, they have to be in the list.

List View has 3 data viewing options. They are key code (default), video, and sound. The viewing options can be selected from the menu at the bottom menu of the list. When key code is selected, the following items appear:

Scene
Take
Roll (Lab Roll Number)
Key code (Key code & key num start)
Length (feet + frames)
Clip name (name of corresponding Quicktime file linked to the record)

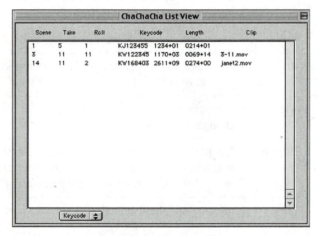

Figure 9.3   The List View

If Video is selected, the List view will show

Scene
Take
Roll (videotape number)
Time code (time code start)
Length (time code format in hours: minutes: seconds: frames)
Clip name (name of corresponding Quicktime file linked to the record)

If Sound is selected, the List View will show:

Scene
Take
Roll (sound roll number)
Time code (time code start on sound roll)
Length (time code format in hours: minutes: seconds: frames)

Clip name (name of corresponding Quicktime file linked to the record)

LINKING MEDIA TO THE DATABASE

In order for FilmLogic to properly function, all of the clips need to be linked to the media so that the relational database is properly established. This not only is necessary for building the database, but is also helpful for finding information about the clips through the database.

Locating and linking clips is relatively easy, assuming that the clips are all located within a single folder. Normally, a clip name consists of the scene and take number. Thus Scene 3 Take 24 would be 3/24.mov or 3-24.mov. So finding the right clips for the right takes is easy. Once FilmLogic has found the clips, it can play them back and display information about the framerate, compression codec, and other tidbits.

Either a group of clips or a single clip can be opened to link to the database. To open a single clip, first load the clip into detail view. Select Find Clip from the right side of the interface. Using standard Macintosh navigation, locate the clip and open it. When the clip opens, note that it immediately becomes linked in the detail view of the database. A thumbnail appears in the lower right corner of Detail View and the name of the Quicktime file appears above it. The file is now linked to that database record. If several files are to be linked, select Find Clips from the Database menu and direct it to the folder where the clips are stored.

Verification

Once the clips are linked, verify burned-in information with the database. With the clip open, click on the Identify button. Specific information about the clip is revealed, including key code prefix, key num, cam roll, format, lab roll, vid TC, sound TC, sound speed and TK (telecine) speed. Verification is one of the key features for FilmLogic. It allows the editor or assistant to verify that the picture information is consistent with the database information. This assures peace of mind, which is what every assistant seeks.

Figure 9.4 The clip menu in FilmLogic

Info

The Info button in the clip window is also helpful for verification. It includes duration, date of recording, codec used, frame rate, audio sampling rate, average data rate and quality of the picture. It can be used to determine frame rate issues with particular clips as well as bandwidth and sound sampling issues for the NLE.

CONFORMING

FilmLogic is loaded with interesting functions. It can conform a picture to its correct time base as well as alter that time base to more accurately reflect a conversion to a 24 fps rate. It all sounds pretty heady, but it's really simple. Quicktime architecture allows for a frame to be any size or duration. Thus, when capturing frames at 30 fps, the duration of each frame is not necessarily 1/30 second. Some Quicktime frames are larger and slower than others. It doesn't seem to make much difference at a 30 fps frame rate, but it does affect a single frame's duration. FilmLogic can change this by conforming a clip to its true time base of 1/30 of a second. The result is more accuracy in conducting frame counts as well as editing.

Even more fascinating is what conform can do for 24 fps PAL films running at 25 fps. By conforming the 25 fps film back to 24 fps, FilmLogic slows the time base down to reflect the more accurate 24fps that will be displayed in the theater. Instead of having to deal with 4.166 percent speed ups and slow downs, 25 fps media can be conformed to 24 fps and still retain frame-to-frame accuracy.

To conform a clip, locate the desired clip in the detail view of the database and select Open Clip. The linked clip will open. To the right of the clip is a column of buttons. Click Conform. There are options to conform the film to 23.98 fps (actually 23.976, the speed of film in a telecine), 24 fps, 25 fps, 29.97 fps or 30 fps. When the clip speed is chosen, select Conform Clip. Remember that conforming a clip cannot be undone. If you're experimenting, make a self-contained copy of the clip to protect the original.

REVERSE TELECINE

Reverse telecine can function in much the same way as conform for NTSC video. By altering the time base and removing pulldown fields, FilmLogic creates a true 24 fps editing environment. Cut lists will match perfectly—no matchback is necessary here because only the 24 original film frames have been retained. Furthermore, by conforming to a true 24 fps, not 23.976 as it is with telecine, the time base is converted to a true 24 fps. The only difference between conforming and reverse telecine is that reverse telecine removes pulldown before altering the time base.

To reverse telecine, click on the Open Clip button in detail view of the clip to be reverse telecined. Select Reverse Telecine from the right-hand row of buttons. If the clip is not digitized at the correct speed, reverse telecine will not work. In order to reverse telecine, the clip frame rate should either be 29.97 or 30.0. PAL projects cannot use reverse telecine. Instead try Conform as mentioned previously.

Reverse telecine can create clips at the following frame rates; 23.98 (actually 23.976), 24 fps, 29.97 fps, 30 fps, and 25 fps. It's also necessary to determine the following information in order to make reverse telecine work properly with the clip: whether the clip is single field or double field; the A, B, C, or D identity of the frame; whether or not the fields are standard upper/lower or vice versa; and whether to create a new independent file or alter the original. The operations guide that came with the digitizing card should show whether the frames are digitized upper or lower first. I personally prefer to create a new file rather than altering the original when I reverse telecine. With some codecs, the quality is compromised. Once those determinations have been made, the clip can be reverse telecined.

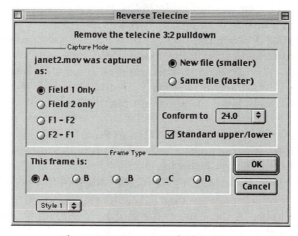

Figure 9.5   Reverse Telecine Menu

Limitations

Although FilmLogic is a very robust database and matchback system, some problems have been reported using Reverse Telecine and Conform on FilmLogic with some versions of NLE applications. Users have lost links to the media files after using reverse telecine. Others have reported that some NLE applications will not use the new time code data properly. All of these issues could very well be fixed, so it's best to consult FilmLogic's website, listed in the Webliography, for current information.

A limitation of reverse telecine is that the time base of the clips inside of the Quicktime-based NLE precludes export of a 30 fps video EDL, but FilmLogic does support 24 fps EDLs. Because the end product is film, this shouldn't pose too many issues. If a 24 fps project is exported to videotape, the videotape will not necessarily perform the pulldown properly. The tape will record whatever frames comprise each second of video, without given durations or intervals for the frame. No fields will be inserted at correct pulldown times. As a result, a frame-to-frame accuracy with respect to pulldown is not guaranteed on an export to tape. However, Final Cut Pro and other Quicktime-based NLEs can use Adobe After Effects plug-ins like the Telecine 3:2 pulldown effect, which can recreate the media at 29.97 fps with pulldown at correct intervals.

When digitizing with Final Cut Pro, be sure to examine the tape to make sure that the burn-in time code window matches the time code that Final Cut Pro captures. If it does not match, the time code Offset might need to be adjusted. Time code offset is located in the capture preferences. Adjusting the offset will ensure that all of the captured frames match time code in the database as well as in the burn-in. This is a small price to pay for an application that can digitize from almost any serial controlled source and most video capture cards.

SOUND CONSIDERATIONS

Telecine rates for film are normally 23.976 fps. If sound is recorded separately from telecine, the adjustment of picture speed must be made to sound. Because the picture is pulled down to the slower rate, sound speed must be slowed .01 percent in order to stay in sync. If the sound speed isn't changed, the result is a slip of one frame every 33 seconds. This could be avoided by inserting a frame of **room tone** every 33 seconds into a synced picture. However, speeding up and slowing down sound in Final Cut Pro is simple, so there's really no need to do this.

To slow down the sound, select Final Cut Pro's Modify menu and choose Speed. Enter 99.99% into the pop-up menu and press Return. The sound speed will now match a standard telecine tape.

If reverse telecine is applied to the picture, the pulldown has been removed and the picture retains true 24 fps original camera speed. As a result, the sound speed recorded should be the same as the picture speed and no speed adjustments should be necessary.

EXPORTING BATCH LISTS

FilmLogic has a lot of considerations when it comes to databasing. Now that everything is databased and sound and telecine speed have been adjusted, it's time to export a **batch list**. With the database open in FilmLogic, under the File menu, select Export, then Batch Capture. FilmLogic exports the information into a batch capture log that can be imported into Final Cut Pro. Batch capture logs can be exported for Edit DV, Final Cut Pro, Media 100, and Premiere.

Importing the Batch Capture Log

After launching Final Cut Pro, it's necessary to import the batch list. Select the File menu, then Import, then Batch List. Using the standard Mac navigation, find the list and import it. The media, if it is not digitized, will appear in the bin with a red slash across its icon. To batch capture, select the File menu and Batch Capture (or choose Command-H).

EDITING WITH FINAL CUT PRO

Edit in Final Cut Pro just like any other video project. Final Cut Pro offers some matte effects for standard film aspects which can be used. Be sure to use lab standard dissolves for 16mm films to save money on opticals. Once the sequence is edited, export the cut lists directly from Final Cut Pro using FilmLogic's cut list plug-in. There is no need to export an EDL for matchback. The plug-in analyzes the data and does all of the work.

Exporting a Cut List

From the File Menu, select Export> FilmLogic Cut List. The menu shown in Figure 9.6 appears.

Most of the list options are standard, with a couple of key differences. Although FilmLogic will not open the databases and flag non-standard or missing key numbers, it will generate a list of missing elements. Missing elements can include any clips that don't contain key numbers or those that might have been databased with incomplete elements from which a cut list cannot be created. If there are any missing elements in the list, it's a fairly simple process to open up the detail view, database the correct information and run the list again.

The other unique option is the creation of a FilmLogic database program. The database program is absolutely essential to creating an audio EDL. Without the database program, it cannot be done. It's highly recommended that a database program be generated with every list. Should any later editing need to be done, all of the elements for re-creating and generating lists are present. When it comes to information on a re-edit, more is better than less.

Table 9.5 shows a list of options available with their descriptions, including the two unique options mentioned previously. FilmLogic creates a text format cut list that can be opened in any text readable application on the computer.

Exporting EDLs

To export an audio EDL, launch FilmLogic, and under the File menu, select Export> Export Audio EDL from Program DB. FilmLogic will ask where the program database is located, then ask where the FilmLogic database is located. Once all of the databases are accounted for, it's time to export an EDL!

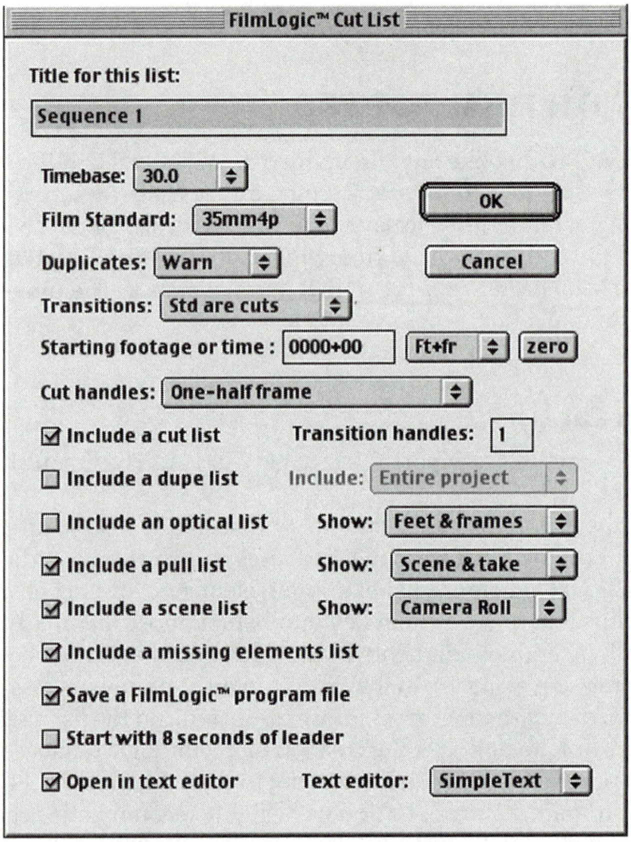

Figure 9.6   FilmLogic Cut List options.

Most of the items in the menu are either preset or self-explanatory. Be sure to select the right text editor for viewing and make sure the time code start point is correct. Once you're ready, take a deep breath and select OK. The result is two separate files: one for notes on the EDL list generation, with any errors noted. The other is the actual EDL. FilmLogic saves the EDL in a text readable file.

FUTURE HOPES

FilmLogic has a robust database that works really well with Final Cut Pro. The company compares their database with a film code book, and I think they're right. The product continues to develop and they frequently post new information on their website, which can be found in the Webliography.

Table 9.5 FilmLogic Cut List Options in Detail

Option	Description
Title for This Sequence	The name of the sequence in the list
Timebase	24, 25, 29.97 or 30 fps
Film Standard	As defined in project settings
Duplicates	Warn or Don't warn if dupes exist in the list. Good to use when checking for dupes before a final list is made.
Transitions	Can be std. or cut for conforming
Starting Footage or Time	Can use feet+frames or time durations
Cut Handles	Handles needed for splicing
Cut List	Selects cut list generation. Be sure to put handles on transitions.
Dupe List	Selects Dupe List generation. Whenever possible, run a dupe list to ensure that costly dupes are kept to a minimum.
Optical List	Selects Optical List Generation
Pull List	Selects Pull List Generation
Scene List	Selects Scene Pull List Generation
Include Missing Elements	Includes elements without Key numbers or other incompletely databased information in the cut.
Save a FilmLogic File	Saves a program database file of the cut that FilmLogic can use for audio EDL generation.
Start with 8 sec. Leader	Adds 8 seconds for SMPTE leader at the head of the reel.
Open In Text Editor	Allows the editor to examine the lists after generation in a preferred text generator
Show	Normally, it's preferred to show feet + frames, Scene & Take, and Cam Roll numbers.

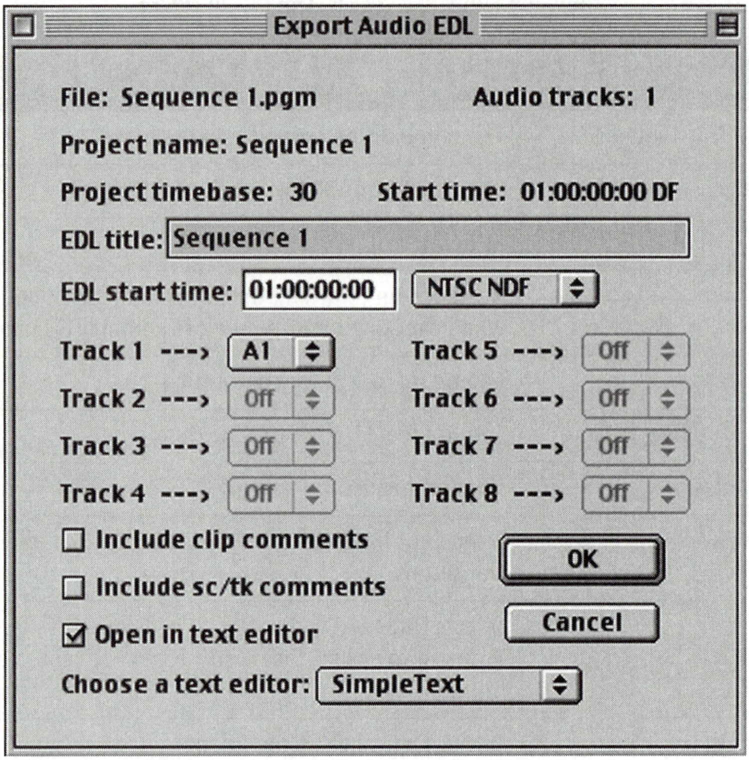

Figure 9.7 FilmLogic Export Audio EDL menu

Chapter 10: Cutting DV for a Film Release

For the creative artist, DV is a great democratizer. It enables filmmakers to shoot projects that they might not otherwise afford. Documentary filmmakers can interview hundreds of subjects. Narrative directors can shoot a take as many times as they want. The cost of DV tape is minimal. It almost seems too good to be true. No synching of dailies, no pulldown issues, and no telecine transfers.

Another advantage is the cost of equipment. DV cameras are very inexpensive. Most of the best prosumer cameras are in a price range between $2,500-$4,500. They offer 3-CCD recording, 16-bit sound, and excellent video imagery. Some cameras have interchangeable lenses, matte boxes and an array of filters. One hundred hours of dailies could cost $800 plus personnel and lights. In the event of a deferred pay production, the savings are phenomenal.

But before you recommend shooting DV to a director, consider some of the limitations of a DV-to-film project.

RESOLUTION

One of the first things mentioned when comparing DV to film is resolution. Is DV the equivalent of 35mm film? Some have suggested that by the time a film is shot, duplicated and run through the projection gate at a theater, it has little more resolution than DV. But usually there is a vested interest in those who say these things. Actually the resolution of DV is nowhere close to that of film. And besides, we're comparing two different processes.

Film is a photochemical process, where light passes through a lens and is projected onto a plane of celluloid which contains a high concentration of tiny silver halide crystals. The crystals are microscopic, ranging in size from .003 to .0003 mil. The size of the crystals is a characteristic of the film, which is defined by the film's speed. These crystals are not uniform in shape, and they are not ordered in a matrix. They are a bunch of crystals painted onto the plane of the film.

Video, on the other hand, depends on a matrix and is uniform in shape, size and order. The image is captured into a prism that separates it into three primary colors. The light sensitive device is photoelectric (as opposed to photochemical) and each one of the photoelectric devices, called CCDs or charged coupling devices, emits a matrix of pixels, which is electronically processed to reproduce that image when joined with the other two corresponding CCDs. Some DV cameras have only one CCD that is sensitive to the entire color spectrum. These are considered inferior to 3-CCD cameras.

A high-quality NTSC DV image consists of about 360,000 viewable pixels. If one were to shoot the same images with a PAL camera, there would be about 420,000 viewable pixels. But shooting with a PAL camera in the United States has some problems. Acquisition of PAL monitors, decks and editing equipment can be difficult and very expensive. As a result, most DV films shot in the United States use NTSC, in spite of the superior picture quality of PAL. (Another great advantage of shooting with PAL is the closeness of frame rate with film, which will be important when transferring to film).

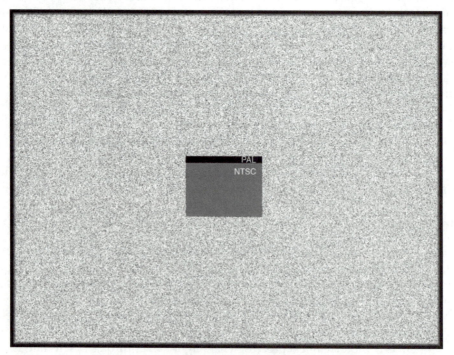

Figure 10.1 The resolution of an NTSC and PAL frame is practically lost when placed in the middle of a 35mm film frame.

How does film compare to that 360,000 pixel image? It's a bit difficult to say, because the silver halide crystals are not counted, nor are they arranged in a mathematically quantifiable matrix. But we get an idea of film's resolution from **film recorders**, high density electronic film scanners used for implementing computer graphic imaging with film, or CGI.

A scanned 35mm frame of film normally consists of 4096 x 3072 pixels. It has the capability of producing an image a little over 12.5 million pixels, a far cry from the 360,000 pixels in a video frame. Thus 35mm film is over 35 times the size (in pixels) of a standard NTSC video frame. To equate this to the big screen, every pixel of video on the screen would equal 35 pixels of 35mm film. To compound the matter, DV is compressed. Although the image is recorded digitally, the information within a DV image is compressed at a 5:1 ratio, adding further resolution issues.

In order to further evaluate the differences between film and video, there is also the need to look at contrast and color space.

CONTRAST

The contrast ratio of any video image is, at best, 150:1. Some would argue that figure to as low as 30:1. Film has a much wider contrast ratio, at about 1,000:1. As a result, a great deal of contrast is lost when using video. The transfer of video to film seems to exaggerate this even more, perhaps because audiences are used to seeing a wider variety of contrasts and tones when viewing films on the big screen. The lack of contrast can result in a decrease of tones and textures within the frame.

COLOR SPACE

In order to properly analyze the differences in color space between film and video, there is a need to examine the process that creates color in video and the spectrum of available colors on film stock.

There is a color gamut of approximately 800 million variations available on film. Different stocks of film are sensitive to different colors. Some pan across the entire spectrum. Others are sensitive to variations in grayscale or luminance. Still others may be sensitive to specific colors. The American Cinematographer's Manual describes the sensitivity of different film stocks to the color spectrum.

Video consists of an RGB signal which must be converted to YUV and then adjusted so that the signal adheres to a standard, such as NTSC or PAL. The process of conversion and the limitation of available color within a video standard severely limits the amount of colors that can be displayed. In order to keep the data size manageable for each image, the color detail is also downsampled.

Let's start with RGB. There are 16.7 million colors in RGB color space. Anyone who has used a paint box or photo application might know that individual colors— red, green, and blue —can be adjusted within a range of 256 levels. (Most photo editing software displays numbers from 0 to 255.) There are 256 levels of each color, which can be used together to create other colors from each channel of color. Thus

256 x 256 x 256=16,777,216

However, the color space becomes limited when considering headroom and footroom available for NTSC and PAL pictures. The video black equivalent of an RGB signal is +16. The white point, or 100 percent luminance, is +235. Anything above or below those luminance levels would be considered a nonstandard video signal. The reduction in levels lowers the available colors to 220. In order to compute the available colors, multiply it much like the previous equation, like so

220 x 220 x 220= 10,648,000

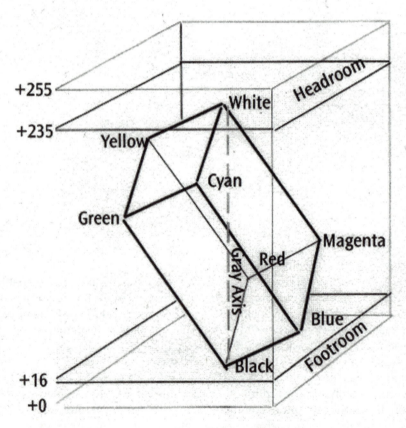

Figure 10.2 Video Signal Color Limitations within the RGB Color Space

After reducing the headroom and footroom, there are 10.6 million colors available in RGB color space. When headroom and footroom limitations are applied to the color space, a rectangle is created like the one contained in Figure 10.2. But the signal also needs to be converted to YUV color space before it can be used. YUV color space is less dense. In his abstract, *Merging computing with studio video: Converting between R'G'B' and 4:2:2,* Charles Poynton mathematically computed the result of the conversion to be 2.75 million usable colors. Others have calculated it to be between 2.6 and 2.75 million. As a result, it can be said that available colors in a video picture are limited to 2.75 million!

The color signal represented by RGB is sampled at 4:4:4. That is, it contains a sampling of luminance information of 4 bits and two samplings of color detail, each with 4 bits of information. In order to make the size of the data more manageable but not too visually different to the human eye, the two color detail components are lowered or downsampled. The human eye has fairly poor color acuity, but can discern luminance variations easily. As a result, the color detail was chosen to make the amount of data more manageable. This compression lowers the color detail from 4:4:4 to the common video standard of 4:2:2 The rate of 4:2:2 color compression is 1.5:1. DV and DVCPro use more compression with lower color detail sampling. DV uses a 4:1:1 sampling while DVCPro uses 4:2:0. The result is a compression in color detail of 2:1. Reduction in color detail sampling can produce artifacts in the picture, including aliasing or "stair-stepping" of elements in the video.

A final limitation of color is this: there are some colors which simply are not available on video, because they do not exist within the color space of 4:4:4 video. Some good examples would be kelly green and a variety of shades of yellow. If a wide variation of color is required for a film, DV is not the answer.

FILMMAKER OR VIDEOMAKER?

Some filmmakers —particularly new ones— are so enthused with the prospect of making a film that they forget to make a plan. Where will it go? How will they market the film? What is the final destination or medium of the work?

Chapter 2 explored several different post production workflows for films. In addition to a workflow, a director needs a marketing plan for the film, particularly a DV film.

Of particular interest to the editor is how and where a film will be displayed. It will either finish on video for direct to tape distribution and video screening at film festivals, or it will finish on film, through some of the processes described later in this chapter.

Why mention marketing plan in a book about editing? Because if the final medium for the film can be determined, the editor can make it look better. The ambiguous intentions of the director can make cutting the film difficult.

Many directors will tell you that they first want to make the video, and if successful, transfer it to film. A lot of independent films are done this way. In fact, it makes sense to do a film this way because all of the inexpensive production costs —shooting on DV and finishing on tape— allow presentation of the work before a relatively expensive transfer to film occurs. Some directors hope that a distributor will pick up the costs of transfer to film.

Most film festivals now allow video projection as well as film. So the expense of showing the work at film festivals is limited to the entry fee. But if an editor can determine the director's ideal intentions, he or she can better prepare the film for screening venues based upon the final product— either videotape or film.

Finishing on Tape

There are a variety of tools that can be used to enhance video to make it look more film-like. The paradox is that none of these tools should be used if the intention is to transfer from DV to film. Before using these devices, the director must make a decision of whether or not the project will finish on film. Once used, these tools can actually degrade the quality of video, making it nearly impossible to obtain a quality video-to-film transfer.

These enhancement tools come in two categories: production tools and post production tools. The production tools are used on the set, while the production is being shot. They consist of special camera filters that can add film-like characteristics to the video. Unfortunately, in order for a filter to work, it must filter something out. The process is always subtractive. So, while it may seem that the look of the video is superior to a non-filtered look, it is always subtracting from the original quality of the video, not adding. Think of it this way: can a filter add resolution to video? Can it add contrast to an image? The answer to both of these is no, but filters can cause the image to appear higher resolution or higher contrast. This is all great and good for video display, but when the DV comes to a video-to-film transfer facility, the artifacts of filtering cause more issues than if the video were shot without any filtering whatsoever.

While directing a documentary in England, I had to make the determination that the final product would be video, not film. As a result, I was able to have my DP use some very good filtering on the images, which look very film-like. But I also realized that this would limit the venue for the documentary to film festivals that accepted DV, and television.

The post production tools for video are plentiful. A very popular filmlook plug-in is made by Digi-Effects. The CineLook plug in uses film stock types and matches the video to presets based upon those stock types. It also is capable of manually being overridden for limited painting of the image. For example, if you want your video image to look like Kodak Vision 200 stock, you can select the preset from an array of stocks and apply it directly to the image in an NLE.

But like camera filtering, plug-in filters are generally subtractive. So while they may appear to be more film-like, it's again better to use the original unfiltered video for a video-to-film transfer.

In addition to filtering, there are some proprietary processes available. These processes necessitate that the video is sent out, much like one would send negatives to a lab for printing. One of them, FilmLook, has been around for a long time. FilmLook was introduced as a solution to make video attain some of the characteristics of film. It's been very popular over the years and I have occasionally edited television with this process included on the video masters. The difference appears to be night and day.

Another consideration is matting. If the director wants the DV to have a 1.85:1 matte as most American made films do, it can be added in the NLE, with black bars at top and bottom. Avid's Film Composer and Final Cut Pro have matte effects that are precise and according to Academy standards. A matte can be applied in any NLE. However, if a video-to-film transfer is intended, a much cleaner matte can be inserted later.

Figure 10.3   Digi-Effects' Cinelook offers several different coloring parameters as well as presets by the manufacturer to emulate different film stocks.

TRANSFERRING FROM DV TO FILM

So, the filters for video produce spectacular results. And video-to-film facilities prefer non-filtered video. If you're not sure where the film is going, what do you do? If time allows, create two sequences of the same cut. Add colorization, filters and mattes to one and call it the video master. The second sequence should be left bare. Call this one the film master. Output both masters to tape. The director can use one for marketing and the other for show. This way, they take advantage of the best of both mediums.

FILMMAKER CONSIDERATIONS

If by chance you are able to discuss the project with the director before principal photography begins, you should make some recommendations that will help the project before it is transferred to film.

- If the filmmaker truly intends to do a video-to-film transfer, he or she should avoid using any lens filters. Lens filtering of any kind tends to distort the image and lowers the resolution characteristics of the video. As previously examined, there isn't a lot of resolution to begin with, so it isn't a good idea to take any more away.
- Although a lot of DV cameras have a 16:9 option, it is recommended that this option not be used. Many cameras accommodate 16:9 by squeezing or distorting pixels. If the DV project is going to be matted, it's better to do it during the film transfer than during shooting. Like filtering, shooting in 16:9 distorts the original resolution.
- Shoot in progressive frame mode, if available. This allows for better picture clarity and motion characteristics more similar to film.
- Shoot in ideal lighting conditions for video, not film. Scenes can be color timed in the final film print, but all of the contrast that video will allow is necessary. Despite its ability to pick up low light images, the flattened contrast ratio of video will negatively affect a video in low light when transferred to film. Blacks do not contrast well in the picture element of dimly lit video like they do in film.
- Do not use the camera anti-shake or stabilizer feature. This slightly enlarges the video image and causes less resolution. Every pixel is needed.
- Shoot farther away from subjects to lower the depth of field. This will give the audience the impression that prime lenses were used instead of video zoom lenses. Depth of field is a dead giveaway that the film was shot in video. Cut down the depth to create a more film-like image.
- As mentioned before, do not use any electronic filtering or proprietary video enhancing processes. Doing so is subtractive from the original resolution and not recommended. Also be sure to not use mattes. Mattes can be inserted onto the film later.
- Cut and output the project using as little compression as possible. Edit the video on an uncompressed video capable NLE if available. Output to digital beta is the most recommended format. Digital beta is more stable than DV tape and is used frequently by video-to-film transfer facilities.

VIDEO-TO-FILM TRANSFER METHODS

To a DV filmmaker, the process of transferring or conforming DV to film is an expensive one. There are many issues surrounding this process that first must be explored. Choosing a method of transfer, usually based upon cost and precision, is the most important. And there are other technical issues to explore as well, such as what will happen to the six frames removed from the video for every second of film that is transferred. There are methods of dealing with this as well.

Once the final cut of a DV film is achieved on an NLE, the video must be transferred to film. There are many ways to do this, including, but not limited to:

Film Recorder

The film recorder scans each frame of film. Payment is based on a per frame basis. It is quite accurate, but very expensive. It usually creates a "2K" picture, meaning a 2000 x 2000 pixel image.

Film Scanner

Film scanners produce extremely high quality scans of electronic images onto film. The most popular image sizes have 2,000 and 4,000 vertical lines of information. These files are known as 2k and 4k respectively. There are two types of film scanner: a laser scanning system that use red, blue and green lasers that scan the image onto the plane of the film and a specialized film camera that scans high resolution monochrome monitors through red, green and blue filters. Laser scanners are costly but produce a superior image. Popular laser systems include Cineon by Kodak, Pthalo Systems Verite, and the Lux system by Digital Cinema.

When film scanners are used, the video is digitized onto a computer and the film recorder sends the images to a film, one frame at a time. Kodak has developed film specifically for this form of transfer.

Kinescopic-like Processes

Similar to the kinescopes of old, these processes create frames from monitor displays of full framed video. Kinescopic processes use high resolution monitors and a specially designed camera to convert the fields to full frames at 24fps. There is no flicker between fields in the process like there have been in previous kinescopes from old television programs. Kinescopes are much less expensive but not the best quality when it comes to transfer.

While similar to CRT film scanners, kinescopic processes use the videotape timebase as a method for creating the film. Whereas film is projected at 24 fps, the resulting kinescope of the video will play back at 23.976. Not as accurate, but much less expensive and usually less time consuming than film recorders.

Electron Beam Recorder (EBR)

Electron beam recorders send an electron beam directly to three different pieces of film for red, green and blue elements of the frame. EBR processes have multiple stages and are less common. They are also less time consuming than film scanning.

A typical EBR process begins with transfer of the video to film with red, blue and green elements separated and then scanned onto three separate pieces of film using an electron beam. The film itself is monochrome, but the separation process sends only those elements relating to each primary color to their respective plane of film. Then the three films are optically printed together using red, green, and blue filtering.

Sony's High Definition Center, one of the facilities on the forefront of video-to-film transfer, begins its EBR process with an upconvert of the video from a standard (SDTV) signal to a high definition (HDTV) format. If the video is not to HD aspect, black bars are inserted on either side. The HD video is then doubled in resolution through a proprietary process before the EBR process is begun. All of the process from up-converting to colorization is HD compliant. Sony Digital and 4MC Inc. are the two primary places for EBR in Los Angeles.

Proprietary Processes

Many video-to-film transfers are done with computers and equipment developed specifically by or for a single company. These systems usually integrate one or more of the previously mentioned processes in order to achieve a final output. Many of the developers of these processes are secretive about how their process works.

Which is right? It's probably best to ask each vendor if a second or two of the video can be transferred as a test. This could cost hundreds of dollars, but a video-to-film print will cost thousands. Better safe than sorry. Once it's determined which process looks best (try projecting the samples at a local theater), determine the total cost of transfer. Some vendors will bargain. As new processes are being developed, they are anxious to get a few credits under their belt. On the other hand, if a well-known vendor is used, bargaining abilities will be limited.

Keep in mind that even though a rough cut can be projected with a video projector, one never knows exactly how good the film will look until the video-to-film transfer is made. If a re-edit is necessary after screening the film print, it's going to cost some serious cash. Video-to-film transfers can cost anywhere from $7,000 to $40,000. Replacing a single edit can lead to even more expense.

DROPPED FRAMES

Another important thing to consider when making a film from DV is the projection speed of 24fps. Video plays 30 frames per second. This means that one out of every five frames must be eliminated in the transfer to film. This could cause some serious problems with movement, but even more so with flash edits. Whenever possible, test, test, test! Try sending samples to vendors to see how they deal with the frame drops. Many processes will blend or interpolate the frames so as not to lose any information. In an interpolated frame, two or more frames are blended together before being transferred to film. Other less expensive processes will drop every fifth frame, which can lead to stuttered pans and tilts as well as important missing frames or single frame cuts (flash cuts) in a montage.

A FILM IS A FILM

Once the video is transferred to film, it can do everything that you would expect of a film. The neg can be color timed, adjusting scene-by-scene or shot-by-shot, and you can duplicate and distribute it like any other film on the market. And the best advantage is that you can store it for long periods of time. You can even take the film and do a recut on a flatbed.

Video retains a reasonably long shelf life, but the magnetic oxide often flakes off, causing **dropout**. Dropout occurs when the scanning head of a videotape recorder hits a blank area of the mylar where no oxide exists. A dropout cannot physically be repaired on the videotape, although there are some solutions with paintbox systems for correcting it. Videotape is also subject to **sticktion**, a name derived from sticky friction. Sticktion occurs when the tape is stored in a hot and humid environment. Although videotape is fairly temperature resilient, it has a tendency to stick together when exposed to hot and humid environments for extended periods of time. Sticktion can ruin a videotape master. Heat and humidity can cause the videotape stock to chemically bond together, making playback impossible.

Perhaps the biggest artifact of videotape is technology. Videotape is limited by the devices which record it. Older television programs show their age by the limitations of the cameras of their day. Streaking lights, low contrast and muted colors are all commonplace in videos of the past. Perhaps this is why over 70% of prime time television is originally recorded on 35mm film.

Film is also affected by time. As the celluloid ages, it can become more brittle. But the most common artifact of film is color fading. The color of a film tends to fade toward magenta after an extended period of time. Magenta film can be restored and properly color timed.

No method of recording; digital, video or film, is timeless. But history has proven that film, with higher definition, more resilient properties, and an absence of the technological limitations of the day, has more longevity than videotape.

Chapter 11:
HDTV, 24p,
and the Future

Writing about the future is dangerous. Time is the test of any predictions, and even the most well-educated guesses can seem ridiculous in the years to come, particularly when it comes to technology. One of my favorite books is a 1950's science work about outer space. The book quotes the scientists of the day, including Arthur C. Clarke, and claims that one day "soon" we will have outposts on asteroids and study Venusian swamp creatures. Computer mogul Bill Gates was once quoted when he asked why anyone would need more than 720K of storage.

With those thoughts in mind, this chapter is not so much a prediction of the future as it is a report of what is here today and might become widely accepted.

THE STANDARD(S)

HDTV (High Definition Television) comes in a variety of flavors. In fact, there are 18 standards. You've probably encountered some of the buzzwords of the HDTV age: 480i, 720p, 1080p, up-convert, down-convert, 16:9 and so forth. So we'll begin by defining some of these new and somewhat confusing terms.

There are three terms which define the format of an HDTV standard. The first is a number which defines the vertical resolution of the picture. The second defines how the picture is stored or displayed. The third defines the frame rate of the images. When the letters *i*, *p*, or *sF* are used, it determines how the frame is stored or displayed. An *i* frame is segmented into fields, as it is in standard television (SDTV) signals used today. A *p* frame is progressive. The frame that is field based is said to be interlaced, hence the *i* suffix. SDTV signals scan every other line of information to form a field (as discussed in Chapter 3) then return to the top of the frame and scan the other lines not scanned in the first field to form a second field. The *sF* frame is a segmented frame, not to be confused with field-based frames. Segmented frames will be discussed later in this chapter.

A progressive frame contains all of the information and is presented on a single temporal frame. The frame that is progressive is non-interlaced, hence the *p* suffix. So a resolution of 1080/24p is a frame that is 1080 horizontal lines and a single progressive frame displayed at a frame rate of 24 fps.

The progressive frame is much like a film frame. It holds all of the elements of an entire picture. Unlike interlaced fields, it does not appear on the screen in succession. When recording a standard television signal, the first field is recorded, then the second field. Further, field-based frames are vertically filtered to prevent small area flicker or "twitter" between the fields. This represents a passing of time for each field or motion phase, which could have different content based upon the moment between fields. For example, if we have a picture of a child kicking a ball, the position of the child's leg in the first field would be different in the second field. This is the nature of field–based imaging. But progressive imaging holds for the entire duration of the frame. There is no interfield motion or jittering when showing an entire frame, because the frame is recorded all at once. When a progressive frame is displayed, all lines of resolution are shown at any point in time. Thus, we could say that a progressive frame is far superior in quality to an interlaced frame.

There are advantages to using a progressive frame when it comes to interformat delivery of SDTV signals, too. Let's consider the common idea of transferring an NTSC picture to PAL. If you're from a PAL country, you're probably frowning about now. There can be nothing uglier than stretching a 525 line frame into 625 lines and eliminating 5 frames per second. It is a jumpy, blurred, and inferior picture.

But if we transferred progressive frames, it would be different. PAL is field based, just like NTSC. Instead of 2 fields of roughly 263 lines, it has two fields of 313 lines— a big difference, for sure. If you then transferred a full frame of 525-line progressive images to field-based PAL format, the resolution artifacts would disappear because 525 lines of resolution would be present at all times in the source via a progressive frame.

The best example of a progressive frame would be your computer's monitor. If you compare the definition of your computer monitor with a conventional NTSC video signal, you'll note that graphics are softer on NTSC. Images that tend to shimmer on NTSC don't have the same artifacts on a computer desktop. And a frozen frame in NTSC will contain motion artifacts. A screenshot of your computer monitor contains no such issues.

So the advent of HDTV has created more alternatives than ever for broadcasters. But in that process, it has created a nightmare for those wishing to create material for a mass audience. Which format should be used?

BANDWIDTH AND FORMAT

The progressive frame presents new bandwidth issues for broadcasters. Now, instead of delivering 60 fields of information, 30 full frames will have to be shown. The broadcasting of full frames creates a need for more bandwidth. But then again, the higher resolution of HDTV demands more bandwidth. The need for more bandwidth is offset somewhat by the frame rate, which is 24 fps.

For broadcasters, HDTV can point to only one thing: compression. Television stations and broadcast companies do not have enough signal bandwidth to recreate an HDTV signal. So, to solve this issue, it is presumed that some, possibly a lot of compression will be necessary. Estimates go as high as 65:1 compression rates and more. This seems to destroy the intent of HDTV in the first place.

For editors, the story is different. As long as machines have the ability to create an uncompressed HDTV picture, that will be the demanded standard. But in its final delivery, what you see may not always be what you get. The issues of the choice of HDTV formats are going to cause considerable headaches for editors. Thus far, the four major U.S. networks have adopted four different HDTV standards (one of the networks is going to use two different standards, and two networks have actually agreed on the same standard—hooray!) As a result, the editing room is going to be a Tower of Babel, where no two videotapes speak the same language.

24p

In the midst of this brouhaha is the need for a universal standard that could potentially be used for upconverting and downconverting of the massive variety of HDTV signals available, according to the needs of broadcasters, filmmakers and producers. Enter 24p, a standard which could not only resolve many of the multiple format issues, but also solve some of the old problems that have been plaguing the video world for years. 24 progressive frame video has a number of advantages, including

- A 1:1 frame correspondence with film without 2:3 pulldown and .01 percent slowdown of audio.
- 24 fps nondrop frame time code.
- The ability to down-convert to SDTV signals such as NTSC, PAL, PAL-M, SECAM and NTSC-J
- High definition 1080p frames, which can be down-converted to 1080i, 780p, 780i, 480p and 480i frames.
- 16x9 frame, which can be panned and scanned, letterboxed, or shown full screen, depending upon the capabilities of television monitors, broadcast bandwidths, and individual needs of the originating broadcast source.
- Less storage space is required to deliver 24 frames per second as opposed to the NTSC standard 30 fps.

1:1 Frame Correspondence with Film

Because of its 24 fps framerate, 24p video has the potential of eliminating all of the pulldown issues associated with transferring film to video. These issues have plagued American television for decades. Combining high definition with a universal standard, 24p can be used as an editing source and a master output source to a variety of formats.

Most prime time television created in the United States is filmed, then transferred to standard NTSC video and edited on NLEs. As a result, a matchback of those edits must be made for overseas distribution. The conversion of an NTSC video signal to PAL is so horrid that most distributors won't accept it. With a 24p universal standard, digital cuts from NLEs could be delivered in most any world standard, including PAL, with no down-conversion artifacts. The result would save extensive labor costs on the conforming and retransfer of the film to PAL.

24 fps Nondrop Frame Time Code

24p uses a 24 fps time code that does not necessitate dropping of frames to establish accurate timing. As a result, the usual issues associated with frame code modes would go away. In fact, 24fps EDLs would allow a worldwide standard of production in which one could shoot in one country and edit in another. EDLs could be used with original transferred or 24p camera masters to recreate content in any country at any time.

This particular concept may seem ordinary, but it isn't. Finding an NTSC cutting facility in Europe can take a lot of research. If 24p becomes the accepted universal standard of recording video and transferring film, the issues of region and format become invisible.

Universal Mastering

Imagine delivering a 480p made-for-television movie for Fox and then later having to recreate it for syndication on late night ABC 1080i television. How could it possibly be done? Using older methods, it would require retransferring the original film and delivery of a new master. But if the original was mastered on 24p, a quick dub of the 24p 1080p master with a down-conversion to 1080i could solve the problem.

This issue becomes even more grotesque in the independent television market. What if you have to deliver reruns of *M*A*S*H* at 480p, 1080i, 720p and 1080p? Telecine and on line would take days at a minimum. All of these issues could potentially go away with the use of a single HDTV 24p standard.

24sF

Although 24p has many advantages, there are some technical drawbacks. Broadcasters and post production companies have sunk thousands of dollars into SDTV formats and will have to bear the brunt of the extra expense that 24p introduces. A variation of 24p has been proposed that might save millions of dollars in conversion costs of videotape equipment. That format is known as 24sF, twenty-four segmented frames per second. 24sF would deliver 24 progressive frames, but they would be stored in a segmented format. That is, information about each frame would be recorded into a pair of divided parts of the frame. By doing this, equipment that normally runs at 60 Hz and 50 Hz (NTSC and PAL, respectively) could easily be adapted to 24sF, which, with two iterations of twenty-four frames, would run at 48 Hz.

It should be noted that a segmented frame is not the same as a field. A segmented frame is a recording of a progressive frame broken into two parts. Therefore, there is no vertical filtering, as with fields, nor is there any motion artifact representing the passage of time, which is characteristic of field based recording. 24sF would reproduce 24p accurately, but would store it in segments.

But like every proposed standard, 24sF has some drawbacks. If the 24sF signal were displayed on an interlaced monitor, the viewer would see significant aliasing, a stair-step artifact which is most apparent on diagonal or curved lines. In order to prevent this, the 24sF picture must be reconverted into a 24p frame before being displayed. In addition, any effects or titling would have the same conversion requirements, because the title or effect would show aliasing artifacts without it.

Monitoring and Flicker

Twenty-four frame video has many of the same problems as twenty-four frame film. To correct issues of flicker with 24 fps film, a double bladed shutter is used in projection. This shutter displays each film frame in two iterations, reducing the flicker artifacts and smoothing the motion. So while film is played back at 24 fps, you see 48 fps, or 24 pairs of duplicate frames. This also poses a challenge for 24p. In order to prevent flicker artifacts, the frames must be reiterated. To compound this problem, the phosphors in a monitor have an instantly decaying nature that would amplify the flicker. Brightness and contrast restrictions on the monitors could restrict the flicker somewhat, but not enough to smooth it out to the human eye. In its native format, a 24p picture would have 24 iterations (24 Hz), each of a different frame. However, to smooth out the process, each frame can be reiterated two or three times (48 Hz or 72 Hz) to eliminate the flicker altogether. But a high definition monitor running at 72 Hz could prove challenging for design engineers.

The 24sF format would solve some of the flicker issues, as it runs at 48 Hz, but there would still be the problem of aliasing artifacts on interlace screens.

Color

As discussed in Chapter 10, the range of color in YUV color space is limited by some estimates to as little as 2.75 million colors. YUV uses a color standard approved by the International Telecommunications Union, or ITU. The specification, called ITU 601, defines the range of color that is used and acceptable for YUV video. The serial digital signal of 24p and other high definition signals uses a new standard from ITU known as ITU-R Rec. 709. This standard is designed for optimal display, just like the 601 standard, but it is different. As a result, conventional SDTV signals and HDTV signals are different with respect to their colors. As a result, any cross-format transfer of film or video will necessarily be monitored on two different monitors for optimal results on each. This could lend itself to the need for more monitors in telecine and editing rooms.

DATACINE

Another possible intermediary for film-to-tape as well as film-to-film is the Data-Cine, developed by Phillips. The DataCine is capable of scanning files up to 2K and storing them on a disk array, using an average of 11 MB per frame. The advantages are many to this form of mastering.

One of the first films to use the DataCine was *Pleasantville*. The images combined black and white and color, using a color correction system by DaVinci Systems on a Phillips Spectre Virtual DataCine. The result was a brilliant effect of selective colorization combined with black and white, which was central to the film. All of the colorization effects were created within the digital domain.

Film images can be transferred from OCN using the Phillips Spirit DataCine scanner. From there, the information is downloaded to the disk array using a high performance parallel interface, or HIPPI. The data amount is huge—up to 350 MB per second. The rate of capture varies, but averages about 6 fps. From there, the information can be controlled by what Phillips terms a "virtual DataCine." This means that the data files can be controlled at telecine speed, 24fps. The advantages of virtual DataCine are many, including:

- It frees up the scanner for transfer of other films.
- The digital data on the virtual telecine can be manipulated like a regular telecine session, using Phillips' Spectre Virtual DataCine.
- The files can be downloaded or converted into any format, including film, HDTV or SDTV
- Color correction and secondary color correction can be implemented for video or film.
- Opticals normally created at the lab can be created on the DataCine and rendered to the disk array.
- No need for dupe lists! The digital information is random access and frames of data can be repeated wherever necessary.
- No worries about neg cutting and the potential destruction of the OCN. The negative is never cut, only transferred to the disk array.
- Direct implementation of EDLs or cut lists to the virtual telecine for direct transfer to film or video. The entire film could be cut on an NLE and the EDL could be sent direct to the DataCine house for conforming digitally.
- All timing or grading of the film is performed digitally using color correction systems.

Many films are attracted to the advantages of DataCine, but there are some minor limitations. The 2K frame size isn't quite the equivalent of film resolution. Phillips readily acknowledges this, but points out that the size of the file approaches diminishing returns after it has reached 2K resolution. And of course, DataCine would not be an interformat solution for video-based mediums. But it has changed the methods of many film producers in that, other than the processing of OCN, a film can conceivably be created in its entirety digitally without a considerable loss of resolution or color and still avoid the lab.

Further developments in transfer machines have been made since Phillips introduced the concept of DataCine. Innovation ITK has created a Millennium Machine which can capture 4K sized frames and is, in their words, "technology proof." Further innovations have been made regarding color systems and data storage. The future clearly rests with film resolution images being manipulated by high tech color systems at faster rates that can be transferred to several mediums for near instant distribution. The age of the digital cinema has truly arrived.

Issues of Cutting and Placement

With every great idea comes a multitude of problems. If you're going to deliver a film to multiple standards, including HDTV and SDTV (Standard Definition Television), how do you cut it?

Somewhere in every great editor's brain is the spark of genius that tells them when to cut. In his book, *On Film Editing,* the late Edward Dmytryk even defines some of the rules of cutting. Ask most editors how they know when to cut, and they'll shrug their shoulders. Most of the rules seem innate.

But they're not. Editors tend to follow lessons learned from viewing too many films and thousands of hours of television. For example, when a subject leaves a frame and reenters in another room in the next scene, we tend to cut when the subject's eyes hit the edge of the frame, and cut to the next scene when the subject's eyes reenter it.

But what happens when you're cutting the same scene to be delivered to both wide and center panned formats? Do you cut when the subject leaves the SDTV frame or wait until it leaves the HDTV frame? Cutting too early for HDTV seems abrupt. Cutting for HDTV will leave SDTV viewers with a stale image and an unintended passage of time. As the subject reenters, the same problems will occur, only inverse. Cutting for HDTV will increase the passage of time and enter the new scene with a stale frame for SDTV viewers. Cutting for SDTV creates an almost comical effect of sped up motion for HDTV viewers.

Another dilemma is the placement of graphics. Do you place graphics within the title safe zone of HDTV or SDTV? Common sense would dictate that you'd want to create two separate masters to avoid graphics flowing off of the screen or odd placement. The ultimate answer would be to cut for HDTV and letterbox for SDTV, but not all producers are going to go for this solution. Thus editors face even more challenging questions as to how they will respond creatively to the problems associated with multiple formats.

For those who choose not to letterbox 16:9 pictures to SDTV, another solution is **pan and scan**. An area fitting the lower resolution format can be chosen to be panned and scanned to create a final picture for that format in the proper aspect ratio. Panning and scanning fills the screen, eliminating the drawbacks of a letterbox. The down side is that you will have to choose what elements of picture are eliminated when panning and scanning.

HDTV NLEs

The inevitable question about HDTV and progressive frame editing is how soon it will begin. The answer is that it has already started, but the transition phase is taking time. Several NLEs are coming on line with HD formats. Avid led the charge in 1999 with its Symphony Universal. But 24p is a fairly unsexy concept and it took a while to take hold.

The Symphony Universal has some limitations. As of this writing, it cannot accept an HD 24p signal, but can recreate a progressive frame. Thus the original 24p master must be downconverted to a standard NTSC videotape before digitization. Through an Avid patented process, the picture is converted into a 24p SDTV format. The final output uses progressive frames and can be made into SDTV PAL or NTSC video.

Figure 11.1 The Avid Symphony Universal with 24p capability.

Avid is moving ahead with newer products, such as the Avid DS HD. This particular product supports 1080p, 1080i, 720p, and SDTV PAL as well as SDTV NTSC signals. You can choose between 24, 25, 29.97, and 30 fps. The Avid DS HD is list compatible with other Avid systems and can convert EDLs and accept OMFI files from other Avids as well.

Pinnacle Systems is also heading into the HD market with its TargaCine video capture card. The TargaCine works with Final Cut Pro and is able, with an optional HDTV tether, to capture 1080/24p, 1080/60i, and 720p formats within a serial digital interface.

Sony has been involved with HDTV since its inception. They provided prototypes in the early 1980s and have been steadily working with development of solutions for broadcasters, video producers, and filmmakers. Currently Sony has a line of HDTV cameras and videotape recorders. As the technology becomes more commonplace, there is little doubt that it will be passed on to the consumer and prosumer markets at lower cost.

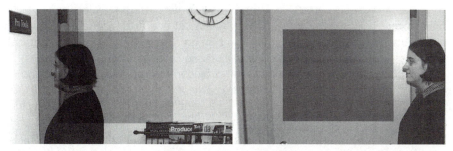

Figure 11.2 A reason for pan and scan. Subject exits through a door and enters another room. If the picture were converted to SDTV from center screen, the editor would want to cut when the subject's eyes left the frame and when they entered the frame in the next shot on the right. If this occurred, the subject would appear to jump from room to room on the wider screen HDTV master. If we waited for the subject to clear the HDTV frame, the SDTV picture would exit and enter the shots "stale" with a lot of empty space between cuts, making continuous action impossible.

24 fps EDLs

Whether you choose Final Cut Pro or Avid as your HD solution, the EDLs created by these machines must support a 24 fps time code to use a 24p source properly. The good news is that 24 fps lists are supported both on Avid's EDL Manager version 10 and FilmLogic version 3. Previous versions of these EDL applications do not support 24 fps time code. For filmmakers, each frame of video corresponds with a frame of film. There are no pulldowns, conversions, sound speed adjustments or reverse pulldowns necessary. 24p lists end all of that. Cut lists are perfect, matchback lists are unnecessary. Both film and video source originate in a tidy 24 frame format.

HDDV CAMERAS?

As 24p increases in popularity, it is assumed that many of the problems associated with creating DV originated films will go away as well. But there are currently no cameras that are cost efficient to allow such a method. It would be cheaper, in fact, to originate an HDTV project on film.

There are a growing number of HD camcorders on the market. Sony, Panasonic and others are working toward a lower-cost solution. Currently, the lowest priced HD camcorders run in the $45,000+ range, but it is likely that there will be an introduction of a lower-cost, less pristine HD solution for low budget filmmakers in the near future. Still, it's doubtful that any $5,000 HD wonders will come around anytime soon to replace conventional DV.

ELECTRONIC CINEMA

As technology evolves, there will no doubt be a means of making 24p HDTV video much more cost effective. When this happens, digital projection is ready. Digital projection may be, in fact, the single most powerful argument for video-based films. It has a lot more capability than any current standards, and might even help to reduce some of the confusion associated with HDTV.

In 1999, George Lucas used digital projection on a limited basis for the release of his film *Star Wars I: The Phantom Menace*. It was displayed via a JVC Hughes ILA-12K projector in some theatres. The frames, all digitally projected from hard drives, were not film or standard video, but CGI, computer generated imagery. The resolution was extraordinary, partially due to the output of the CGI, but also due to the projection power of the ILA. The JVC Hughes projector has the capability of displaying 17,000 lumens with resolution greater than 2000 lines and a contrast ratio that exceeded 1500:1. Compared to SDTV and even 35mm film, it is clear that digital electronic cinema projection is here to stay.

Table 11.1 Resolution/Contrast Comparison of SDTV, Digital Projectors and 35mm Film

	Vertical Pixels	Contrast Ratio
SDTV	480	150:1
Digital Projection	1536	1500:1
35mm Film	~3072	1000:1

Well on the warpath toward achieving film resolution, JVC and other companies are pressing the technological envelope to develop even higher resolution for their projectors. JVC recently developed a single panel projection system capable of delivering twice the horizontal pixels of the HDTV spec.

The proposed next step for JVC has been tentatively called Q-HDTV. Q-HDTV will have four times the pixel density of the HDTV ITU Spec (1290 x 1080), delivering a whopping 3840 x 2160 image at a 16:9 aspect ratio. The future of digital cinema could potentially exceed the resolution of 35mm film. And based upon the spec for JVC's single plane Digital ILA device, it is certainly possible.

Although the numbers indicate a marked difference in vertical resolution, it could be said that the normal projection of film, with gate jitter and similar artifacts, narrows the gap between Q-HDTV and 35mm significantly. In the case of D-ILA projection, JVC claims that the engineering of their systems allows for zero pixel artifacts.

Table 11.2   Future Shock: Proposed Q-HDTV Projection vs. Video & Film

Format	Vertical Pixels	Contrast Ratio
SDTV	480	150:1
HDTV	1080	>150:1
Q-HDTV	2160	1500:1
35mm	~3072	1000:1

The development of such powerful projection systems creates more questions than it answers. How will production equipment manufacturers respond? Will there be a new standard for video that exceeds current HDTV formats? No one can be sure. But for those creating animation or CGI, the possibilities for digital projection already seem endless. Without the need of film recorders, CGI films can be rendered, transferred, and projected almost immediately.

Cost will certainly play a major role in the acceptance of digital projectors. Currently, the very best systems on the market run into the hundreds of thousands of dollars. This is not a very pretty scenario for those operating a local Bijou. But as development increases, costs go down.

Another factor is size. Many manufacturers are increasing the size of their projectors to increase resolution. A lighter and more compact system would be more desirable for smaller digital cinemas and for industrial and corporate use. Many digital projectors are already on the market for much less money, with a lot less firepower. Prices tend to hover in the low five figures, but will no doubt drop over time.

SUMMARY

In the original preface to his 1953 book, Fahrenheit 451, Ray Bradbury envisioned a day when teenagers would tune out the world by attaching radios to their heads, where crazed drivers would maim and kill on our roads for thrills, and where people would be addicted, even mesmerized, by picture wall screens in their homes.

The future of electronic film is closer than most people think. With HDTV, digital broadcast and high quality digital projection systems coming on line, there might be a niche in the market again for Mom and Pop local Bijous with limited seating and plenty of atmosphere. One wonders whether we'll return to the cozier settings of the theater from years gone by.

But then again, if the prices continue to plummet on technological advances, the theater might be in our own homes, as Bradbury predicted. And the biggest fears of filmmakers during the 1950's may come true: we might all be sitting around in our homes looking at wall screens.

Glossary

A neg — Exposed negative that is telecined and used for cutting. A neg comprises the circled takes on a production.

A-roll — Also referred to as single strand conforming. A method of conforming a single strand of negative, used primarily for 35mm film.

Aaton code — A type of time code used in Aaton cameras. Aaton code is accurate to within a tenth of a second, but readable only through Aaton Keylink telecine database systems.

Aaton file — A telecine log format whose suffix ends with .flx. Also known as a flex file.

A/B strand conforming — Also referred to as dual strand conforming. A method of conforming two strands of negative, used primarily for 16mm film.

Absolute frames — A method of measuring film, as opposed to footage+ frames. Absolute frames do not count feet. Thus a 35mm footage count of 1+00 would be 16 in absolute frames. Used commonly by animators and CGI.

Academy leader — Leader placed at head of release prints, counting from 11 to 3. As opposed to SMPTE leader.

Acmade — A company that manufactures ink number printers used for reference along the edges of film and mag stock. Used when conforming workprint and mag stock. Not commonly used with NLEs, Acmade numbers can be entered into Avid Film Composer databases. Acmade numbering systems have two leading characters for 16mm film and three leading characters for 35mm, followed by 4 or 5 footage count numbers, as in AA -10256. These were developed originally for the English method of shot counting vs. scene numbering.

ALE Avid Log Exchange — A format used for converting telecine files. Also an application for converting telecine files created by Avid Technology. ALE is used as a log import format for Avid and other NLEs.

Ambience — Also referred to as room tone or presence, production sound used where there is no dialog to establish a setting. More traditionally, ambience refers to outdoor locations, room tone refers to interiors.

Aspect ratio — Ratio of picture width to picture height. 1.85:1 is the most common film aspect ratio in the United States, 1.66:1 is more common in Europe. Standard definition television is 4:3. Most HDTV pictures are 16:9.

Assemble list — Also known as the cut list. A cut list that includes all the edits in a sequence in the order in which they occur chronologically. Used for conforming negative or work print.

ATSC — Advanced Television Standards Committee. The group that is developing standards for high definition and digital television as well as compression schemes for broadcasting them. Currently there are 18 different types of HDTV.

Autosync — Feature that allows for synching and combining of audio and picture clips on an Avid NLE.

B neg — Exposed negative that is usually not telecined. Non-circled takes.

Balancing — The process of creating and maintaining a footage balance between cut reels. Reels used for screenings normally are 1000 feet long. Balancing the reels maintains consistency is length without interrupting the flow of the film.

Batch digitize — The automated process of digitizing previously logged clips in a batch on NLEs.

Batch list — Import log format for Final Cut Pro. A telecine log must be converted into a batch list before it can be digitized into a Final Cut Pro NLE. The equivalent of an ALE file for Avid or Power Log file for Media 100.

Best light transfer — A method of telecine transfer where each scene is corrected to look its best, without consideration of continuity of color between scenes, as in a scene by scene transfer.

Bin — A container where workprint is stored hanging from pins. The editor's completed scenes are normally stored in a separate bin. A bin normally consists of a series of hooks that overhang into a nonfibrous bag. The clips are attached to cardboard trim tags that visually identify the scene, take, edge numbers, and a short description. The tags and clips are hung on pins and cascade into the bag. Should one of the clips fall off of a hook, you are immediately introduced to the film editor's sport of bin diving. NLEs have virtual or electronic bins, where pointers to media files are located. NLE bins are used in much the same way as film bins, with the added feature of the ability to copy clips into several different type bins.

Bin diving — The act of having to fish out or find a clip that has fallen into the bin.

Bleach bypass — Popular lab technique used to reduce contrast and desaturate color in a film.

Blow-up — The process of optically enlarging the scale of an original frame, a method of increasing the scale of the frame to show only a part of the original. Also can refer to the process of enlarging a film from one gauge to another, i.e., blowing up a 16mm film to 35mm film. Could also refer to an editor when too many changes are made.

Burn-in — Refers to character generated numbers superimposed on video telecine transfers. Typical burn-ins would include video time code, audio time code, and key numbers.

CCD — Charged Coupling Device. Photoelectric device that converts light into an electronic signal in a camera. Professional video cameras use 3 CCDs.

Camera roll — A roll of motion picture film used in production, usually 400 feet or 800 feet in length. Each roll is assigned a unique number for reference. Also called cam roll.

Camera report — A report issued for each camera roll by the camera department of a motion picture production. Includes scene numbers, takes, circled takes, footage and other information. A copy of this multi-carbon form should be sent to the editorial department.

Capture — To input video and/or audio into an NLE format. Also known as digitizing.

Change list — A list of instructions comparing an updated cut of a sequence to its previous version. Simplifies changes for the person conforming by only listing updated revisions and new edits.

Changeover — The point where the projectionist switches between reels during display of a motion picture. Changeover cue marks must be made 24 frames before the last frame of action (LFOA).

Circled takes — Refers to method of circling takes that the director wishes to print during production. Takes are circled on camera and sound reports as well as on facing pages in the script supervisor's notes. When referring to the film, circled takes are also known as the A neg. Non-circled takes, not normally telecined, are called B neg. These terms are not to be confused with A roll and A/B roll methods of conforming film.

Clapper — The two striped sticks used on a slate that aid in establishing sync on a shot. By clapping the two sticks together, visual and aural reference for sync is established on film.

Clip name — A name given to a shot used in an NLE to identify it. Clips are usually named after a scene and take number, i.e., "16/1" for scene 16 take 1.

CMX — The most common format for EDLs, CMX was one of the first computer controlled editing machines and a pioneer in nonlinear editing machine development. CMX 3400 EDLs have 2 audio tracks, CMX 3600 have 4. Originally a co-venture of CBS and Memorex.

Color correction — The process of adjusting film colors using a colorization system. A component of telecine.

Colorist — Talented artist in telecine who adjusts the color for each shot. Also incorrectly referred to as a telecine operator.

Color timing — Also called timing or grading. The process of adjusting color balance for each scene from a conformed negative.

Composite print — A positive print that has both picture and sound. Also called married print.

Conform — To assemble workprint or negative according to a list, usually a cut list. The term has been expanded to refer to assembly of a videotape sequence from an EDL or an audio sequence from an EDL. Can also refer to assembling an on line high quality video finish from an offline video edit, as in "on line conforming."

Continuity reports — Could refer to notes made by a script supervisor regarding script continuity. Also refers to reel continuity, where an editor reports durations of reels, last frame of action and last frame of film.

Cut list – An EDL for film. Instead of time code numbers, edge numbers are used.

Dailies — The results of a single day of shooting. Usually refers to workprint made from a single day of shooting, but can also refer to a videotape transfer of the footage. Referred to as dailies because of the traditional method of shooting, developing and printing overnight. Same as rushes.

DAT — Digital Audio Tape. Audio tape recording format used by many sound recordists and audio engineers. SMPTE DAT is most commonly used.

Datacine — A telecine capable of scanning and creating large image files that go beyond the constraints of SDTV video. Datacines can be used for storing color corrected frames of film and the files they create can be scanned back onto film, avoiding the need for color timing.

Digital cut — A video output of your project direct from an NLE

Digitize — Also known as digitalize in some European circles. To input video and/or audio into a digital NLE format. Also known as Capturing.

DNR — Digital Noise Reduction. An option used in telecine that can virtually eliminate all sources of noise on the film. Potentially hazardous to use, as it can also remove grain, which might be desirable.

Double strand — See A/B roll.

Drop frame — a time code counting method that reflects real time. In order to compensate for the base 30 time code count and the actual frame rate of NTSC video (29.97 fps) drop frame time code skips ahead two frames in the count at the top of every minute, excepting the tenth minute of time.

DTV — Digital television. DTV is a standard for broadcast that incorporates transmission of a digital signal vs. traditional analog. Often confused with HDTV, which is a format.

Dual strand — See A/B roll.

Dupe — A duplicate. When one or more frames are used twice in an edited sequence. Short for "duplicate", as in duplicate frames. Dupe lists are generated to determine which frames will need to be duplicated before a list is conformed. The neg is copied onto an interpositive, which is then duplicated (see IP).

Dupe list — A list of frames that need to be duplicated before conforming a cut list. Dupe lists are checked frequently during editing to prevent the high cost of duplicating negative.

Edge code — A broad classification of film frame numeration which could be either Key Numbers or Ink Numbers. Printed numbers on the edge of film that identify frames; a method of keeping track of edits through a simple numbering process. There are two types of edge numbers. Acmade or ink numbers can be printed on the edge of synced workprint and mag track by an inkjet printers. Key numbers (also called latent edge numbers) appear on the edge of the film when it is developed. Key numbers are more commonly used with NLEs.

Edit bench — The place where much of the nondigital work takes place. Synching and conforming are done here. Also known as "the bench" or work bench. Typically contains rewinds, a gang sync and a splicer.

EDL — Edit Decision List. A list of edits in a sequence showing time code numbers for both source and record tapes. Used for Online video editing, sound conforming, spotting and mixing and in some cases, for comparison with telecine logs for matchback. Can be used with some computerized video editing equipment for automatic conforming.

EOP – End of Picture. The very last frame of projectable film on a reel. Usually occurs a second or more after the LFOA to accommodate for human error when switching between reels. Also known as LFOP, Last Frame Of Picture.

Evertz — A manufacturer of motion picture equipment. Also refers to a telecine log format whose files end with an .ftl suffix.

Facing pages — Pages printed on the back of 3-hole punch paper used in conjunction with a script so that the editor can see both script pages and script supervisor notes. Contain scene, take, camera and other details recorded while on location.

Flatbed — A film editing system for playing back conformed workprint. Flat beds are flat tables with viewing screens attached. Most common are KEMs and Steenbecks.

Flat transfer — A telecine transfer where color and luminance are kept in the middle ranges. Flat transfers are used for footage that will be color corrected later in the post production process.

Flex — Also known as "flex files" or Aaton files, a telecine log format whose files end with an .flx suffix.

4:2:2 — Also 4:4:4, 4:1:1, 8:8:8 and others. Sampling rates used in digitizing video images. The higher the number, the better the sample. Higher numbers also create more cumbersome file sizes and complex pictures. The first number refers to the luminance of the picture. Second and third numbers refer to color. Sometimes a fourth number is also included, which refers to a key or alpha channel.

fps — Frames Per second. Used to measure video or film playback rates.

Frame handles — See Handles.

Gang sync— A gang synchronizer. Used to synchronize picture with one or more sound tracks on an edit bench. Measures footage and frames.

Grading — Also called timing or color timing. The process of adjusting color balance for each scene from a conformed negative.

GVG — Grass Valley Group. A manufacturer of video and television production equipment. Also an EDL file format. GVG EDLs usually refer to their software versions. Most commonly used are 4.0—7.0.

Hamburger — Slang for the Fast Menu used to access preview mattes in an Avid.

Handles — The number of extra frames required for splicing, usually when conforming the OCN. With some splicers, adjacent frames are destroyed during conforming. By adding a number of frames as a handle in your cut list, you can determine whether or not adjacent frames need to be used in other edits, which would require a dupe.

Hard matte — Term used when shooting OCN with a matte in place. As opposed to a soft matte, where no physical matting is done during the production phase.

HDTV — High definition television. One of several formats created for the production of higher quality video images, beyond the normal range of SDTV.

Ink numbers — Also called Acmade Numbers. Inkjet numbers that are added to a workprint and mag stock for reference. Can be used in some NLEs. Also used for Preview Code. Key Numbers are more commonly used for digital editing.

Interlock projector — The projector used for screening workprint and dailies. It consists of a film projector and mag track player that can be "interlocked", thus remain in sync.

IP — Interpositive print. Created from the OCN, this positive print is used to duplicate a negative. IPs are created for items on a dupe list.

ITU — International Telecommunications Union. An international committee that adopts standards for television, including HDTV. The ITU standard for HDTV is 1920x1080, with no frame rate specified.

Jutter — Also called judder. A stopping and stuttering motion of video caused by pulldown in the telecine process. 2:3 produces the most telecine jutter. PAL B pulldown produces very little.

Key code — Refers to the barcode reference which is machine readable and is placed adjacent to key numbers on a film. Key code can be read by a telecine to generate a database of numbers during a telecine transfer. Commonly confused with key numbers.

Key code reader — A machine used in telecine that reads the latent bar code on film. Key code readers are located on the telecine scanner, usually connected to a character generator which can put key number burn-in windows onto a transferred videotape.

Key numbers — Latent edge numbers that appear along the edge of the film near the sprocket holes. The numbers are adjacent to Keykode, a bar code system used in telecines to identify the frames. Not to be confused with Ink or Acmade numbers, which are printed on the edge of film after the film is processed. Key numbers are generally used for digital editing more often than ink numbers.

Keyscope — A telecine log format using files that end with .ksl.

Lab roll — A roll of negative stored in a lab configuration. Most lab rolls are 2000' and consist of combined camera rolls.

Lab standard durations — The standard durations for opticals of A/B conform films that can be created by the lab, thus bypassing more expensive optical print. The lab standard durations are 16, 24, 32, 48, 64 and 96 film frames.

Leader — Film-like materials that are attached to head and tail of a reel of film. Clear leader is used as a protecting agent and threading guide for a reel and is attached at the head and tail. Picture leader contains writing that identifies the reel and its contents. Picture leader is usually placed at head and tail. SMPTE or Academy leader provides a countdown before the picture content of a film begins. SMPTE or Academy leader is placed at the head of a reel adjacent to picture content.

LFOA — Last Frame of Action. The last frame of action intended for projection on a given reel. The LFOA is preceded by motor start and changeover cues.

LFOP— Last frame of picture. The very last frame of projectable film on a reel. Usually occurs a second or more after the LFOA to accommodate for human error when switching between reels. Also known as EOP, End Of Picture.

Lined script — A script prepared by the script supervisor, marked with vertical lines to determine coverage of a shot, indicating which characters are on camera for a given take at a given time. Used by editors for easy reference.

Lok box — Also known as a lock box. A videotape player connected to a gang sync, used for conforming a negative. Can also refer to the output of an NLE to videotape which is used for conforming.

Log — The entering of information about clips which could include time code, key numbers and so forth. Can also refer to a medium on which the logging data is placed, such as a file or paper. (See Telecine Log)

Mag stock — Sometimes, but not always, used with dailies, mag stock (aka mag track) is magnetic audio tape attached to a plastic backing which resembles film and consists of sound portions of the film. It is normally synced on an editing bench with the dailies, which are projected for the director to look at and make notes. Mag stock is cut with workprint on flatbed and upright film editing machines. For digital purposes, mag stock and workprint are used to conform a film.

Married print — A positive film print with both picture and sound.

Matchback — A process which allows generation of a film cut list from a 30 fps video based project. Matchback lists can be + or – 1 frame accuracy per edit. A method of converting from one framerate to another, i.e., from 30 fps video to 24fps film. Matchback provides ease of use with the ability to generate both EDLs for video and Cut Lists for a telecined film. Commonly used process for television where a conformed print will be required for distribution in other formats. Could also refer to the application which generates a matchback list.

Meta speed — An option used on Cintel telecines that allows for an extraordinary variety of frame rates during telecine transfers. Meta speed transfers can range from -30 fps to +96.

MOS— From German, "mit out sound". A scene that is without sound.

Motor start — A cue given to the projectionist as to when to begin running the motor, but not the projection lamp and sound head, on a second projector before a changeover occurs. Motor start cues must be given 200 frames (8 seconds) before the last frame of action (LFOA)

Mute Print — A print with no sound. Picture only print.

NLE — A term for Nonlinear Editor. A digital computer system application that features editing in a nonlinear method. Also known as DNLE or Digital Nonlinear Editor. Manufactured by Avid Technology, Media 100, Lightworks, Apple (Final Cut Pro) and others.

Nondrop frame — A time code counting method that reflects 30 fps instead of the more accurate 29.97 fps of NTSC video. As a result, this method of counting frames is not duration accurate, but each number correctly accounts for each frame without skipping ahead, as drop frame does. See Drop frame.

NTSC — National Television Standards Committee. The group that developed the standard for color television in the U.S. NTSC signals have 525 lines of vertical resolution at a rate of 29.97 fps.

OMFI — Open Media Framework Interchange. A file format that is used primarily for transferring audio files and sequences from one work station to another. Platform independent.

One light — A non-timed exposure of the OCN to a positive copy of the film. It is not the prettiest copy of the film, but presentable.

One light telecine — Also called a "Lab transfer." A telecine transfer done with color correction "on the fly", used for editing purposes. Much less expensive than a best light transfer or a scene by scene telecine.

Opticals — The separate creation of dissolves, fades and superimpositions by an optical house. A-Roll conformed films must create opticals of all such effects. A/B roll conformed films must create opticals of any effects that are not lab standard durations.

Original camera negative (OCN) — The original film shot on location. Most films are shot with negative (not reversal) film.

PAL — Phase alternating line. Standard (as opposed to NTSC) used in many different countries. Features 625 vertical lines of resolution and 25 fps.

PAL telecine A — The method of transferring film shot at 24 or 25 fps to PAL videotape via telecine running at 25 fps to achieve a 1:1 frame ratio with the OCN. PAL A telecine shot at 24 fps will have a speed increase of 4.166% when played back on videotape. Some NLEs have speed correction capabilities to adjust it back to original shooting speed.

PAL telecine B — The method of transferring film shot at 24fps to 25 fps PAL video, using a pulldown field every 12th frame to adjust the timebase so that the two match in duration, but not frame for frame accuracy. PAL B has all of the trappings of NTSC 2:3 pulldown, but with less frequency. Also known as 25@24.

Pan & scan — A method of transferring wide screen images to SDTV, where the telecine operator can zoom into a part of the widescreen image and pan across it, filling the SDTV screen, but eliminating some elements of the wider original picture. Pan and scan is a time consuming and expensive method of transfer.

Picture leader — Placed adjacent to SMPTE or Academy leader, picture leader has information written on it that consists of project name, reel number and running time.

Power log — Import log format for Media 100. A telecine log must be converted into a batch list before it can be digitized into a Media 100 NLE. The equivalent of an ALE file for Avid or Batch List for Final Cut Pro.

Pull list — a type of list sorted usually be source, i.e., camera roll, so that the person conforming neg or workprint can pull each shot from that roll at one time prior to assembling the cut.

Preview code — Ink code reference that applies to changes on a conformed work print.

Reddy-Eddy — A circular gauge used in film cutting rooms that calculates film footage to running time and vice versa.

Reversal — Film stock that produces a positive image and requires no printing, as opposed to negative.

Reverse telecine — The process of removing pulldown fields in an NLE so that the digital picture matches the OCN at a 1:1 frame for frame ratio. Process can occur either during or after digitization, depending upon configuration.

Rewinds — Devices used for winding rolls of film backward and forward on an edit bench.

Rivas — a butt splicer commonly used in film editing rooms.

Roller splicer — film splicer manufactured by CineTrim. Uses a round blade to cut film in an unobtrusive manner which is safer for careless or left-handed editors.

Room tone — Also referred to as ambience or presence, production sound used where there is no dialog to establish a setting. More traditionally, ambience refers to outdoor locations while room tone refers to interiors.

Rushes — The results of a single day of shooting. Usually refers to workprint made from a single day of shooting, but can also refer to a videotape transfer of the footage. Referred to as rushes because of the traditional method of shooting, developing and printing quickly for editorial use. Same as dailies.

Scanner — Also known as a film scanner, flying spot scanner or telecine scanner. The physical machine where the film passes through a scanner and is converted to video.

Scene by scene telecine — a method of telecine transfer where color is carefully corrected for best exposure of a film and continuity between scenes is also carefully calibrated. Unnecessarily expensive for editing, a scene by scene is sometimes used after a cut has been made of a film for video distribution or promotion.

Script supervisor — The person responsible for maintaining script notes and circled takes. Produces facing pages and notes for editing.

SDTV — Standard Definition Television. Refers to current television standards, such as PAL, NTSC, PAL-M and SECAM. As opposed to HDTV, High Definition Television.

Sequence — Another term for an edited master, cut or program created in an NLE.

Short end — Term for a short roll of film, typically cut off for use on another shoot. Commonly used on low budget projects.

Single strand — Also referred to as A-Roll conforming. A method of conforming a single strand of negative, used primarily for 35mm film.

SMPTE — Society of Motion Picture and Television Engineers. A society that develops standards used for television and film.

SMPTE DAT — A digital audio tape (DAT) machine that uses SMPTE time code. SMPTE DATs are far more expensive than a conventional non-time code DAT.

SMPTE leader — Countdown leader placed at the head of each built film reel. SMPTE leader counts from 8 to 2 seconds. When the first "2" frame appears, a 1000 Hz tone pops with it (called the 2-pop or sync pop) and an additional 47 frames of black are shown before the reel starts. As opposed to Academy leader, which counts from 11 to 3.

SMPTE time code — The time code standard approved by SMPTE, as opposed to other standards such as VISCA time code. The most commonly used format of time code.

Soft matte — Term used when shooting without a matte, with the intention of inserting one during negative printing. Soft matting allows for adjustments to be made to the frame optically if necessary. Also allows for a 1.33:1 aspect frame to be displayed on videotape or DVD.

Sound report — A report issued for each sound roll by the sound department of a motion picture production. Includes scene numbers, takes, circled takes, SMPTE time code, and other information. A copy should be sent to the editorial department.

Sync pop — A 1000 Hz tone emitted for one frame 47 frames before a reel begins. Used to establish sync with a SMPTE leader "2" frame. Also called a 2 pop.

Take— The filming of a single shot.

Telecine — The process of transferring film to videotape. A telecine maintains a consistent relationship between film and video frames. Not to be confused with a Film Chain, which is not as accurate.

Telecine log converter — An application within Trakker's Slingshot™ matchback suite. Converts telecine files to NLE usable import files. Could generically refer to all telecine log converters as well, including Avid Log Exchange.

Telecine logger — A computer system used to database the relationship between key code from an original camera negative to video time code recorded on a telecine transfer videotape.

Three perf — A 35mm system that records a single frame using only 3 perfs instead of the traditional four. Used mostly for television production, three perf requires a specially equipped camera and a telecine with meta-speed or other speed alteration device.

Time code — A numbering system used to measure frames of video. Nondrop frame is most commonly used on film, has a direct number to frame correspondence but is not completely time accurate due to the actual video rate of 29.97 fps (NTSC). Drop frame does not have a direct frame to frame numbering correspondence but is time accurate.

Time code reader — A machine used in telecine that reads time code, usually connected to a time code character generator which can put time code burn-in windows onto a transferred videotape.

Time logic control — A method of transferring film to videotape where the pulldown remains consistent between stop points or edits. If a telecine stop occurs on an A frame, the next recorded frame will be a B frame. Commonly referred to as TLC, not to be confused with Slingshot's TLC or Telecine Log Converter files.

Timing — Also called grading or color timing. The process of adjusting color balance for each scene from a conformed negative.

Trim tab — A small white tab that indicates the content of a clip in the trim bin. West coast trim tabs are usually rectangular. On the east coast, they prefer cross shaped tables.

2:3 pulldown — The process in telecine created when a film, shot at 24 fps, is transferred to video at 30 fps. Every other frame of film is held for an extra field of video, thus the fields run in a 2:3 order. Used in NTSC telecine only.

2 Pop — A 1000 Hz tone emitted for one frame 47 frames before a reel begins. Used to establish sync with a SMPTE leader "2" frame. Also called a sync pop.

Upright — A vertical viewing system for film. Also used for cutting. Moviolas are the most common uprights used. Vaguely resembles a sewing machine with two pedals attached, one for sound, the other for picture.

Wild lines—Dialog that is recorded without the camera rolling.

Wild sound — Sounds that are recorded without the camera rolling.

Window burn-in — See Burn-in.

Workprint — Positive prints (workprint) of film created from the OCN. They usually consist of only the takes that the director orders printed. (Hence the director's on-location phrase "Print it!") Workprint is disposable and used for editing. It gets cut, hung in a bin, spliced and unspliced together, cursed at and abused. If destroyed, it can be reordered from the lab. If additional takes need to be printed, the editor can order them from the lab.

Appendix A: Time/Footage Conversions

Min:Sec	35mm	16mm		Min:Sec	35mm	16mm
00:01	1.5	0.6		01:00	90	36
00:02	3	1.2		02:00	180	72
00:03	4.5	1.8		03:00	270	108
00:04	6	2.4		04:00	360	144
00:05	7.5	3		05:00	450	180
00:06	9	3.6		06:00	540	216
00:07	10.5	4.2		07:00	630	252
00:08	12	4.8		08:00	720	288
00:09	13.5	5.4		09:00	810	324
00:10	15	6		10:00	900	360
00:11	16.5	6.6		11:00	990	396
00:12	18	7.2		12:00	1080	432
00:13	19.5.	7.8		13:00	1170	468
00:14	21	8.4		14:00	1260	504

00:15	22.5	9		15:00	1350	540
00:16	24	9.6		16:00	1440	576
00:17	25.5	10.2		17:00	1530	612
00:18	27	10.8		18:00	1620	648
00:19	28.5	11.4		19:00	1710	684
00:20	30	12		20:00	1800	720
00:21	31.5	12.6		21:00	1890	756
00:22	33	13.2		22:00	1980	792
00:23	34.5	13.8		23:00	2070	828
00:24	36	14.4		24:00	2160	864
00:25	37.5	15		25:00	2250	900
00:26	39	15.6		26:00	2340	936
00:27	40.5	16.2		27:00	2430	972
00:28	42	16.8		28:00	2520	1008
00:29	43.5	17.4		29:00	2610	1044
00:30	45	18		30:00	2700	1080
00:31	46.5	18.6		31:00	2790	1116
00:32	48	19.2		32:00	2880	1152
00:33	49.5	19.8		33:00	2970	1188
00:34	51	20.4		34:00	3060	1224
00:35	52.5	21		35:00	3150	1260
00:36	54	21.6		36:00	3240	1296
00:37	55.5	22.2		37:00	3330	1332
00:38	57	22.8		38:00	3420	1368
00:39	58.5	23.4		39:00	3510	1404
00:40	60	24		40:00	3600	1440
00:41	61.5	24.6		41:00	3690	1476

00:42	63	25.2		42:00	3780	1512
00:43	64.5	25.8		43:00	3870	1548
00:44	66	26.4		44:00	3960	1584
00:45	67.5	27		45:00	4050	1620
00:46	69	27.6		46:00	4140	1656
00:47	70.5	28.2		47:00	4230	1692
00:48	72	28.8		48:00	4320	1728
00:49	73.5	29.4		49:00	4410	1764
00:50	75	30		50:00	4500	1800
00:51	76.5	30.6		51:00	4590	1836
00:52	78	31.2		52:00	4680	1872
00:53	79.5	31.8		53:00	4770	1908
00:54	81	32.4		54:00	4860	1944
00:55	82.5	33		55:00	4950	1980
00:56	84	33.6		56:00	5040	2016
00:57	85.5	34.2		57:00	5130	2052
00:58	87	34.8		58:00	5220	2088
00:59	88.5	35.4		59:00	5310	2124
01:00	90	36		60:00	5400	2160

Bibliography

Bancroft, David. Digital High Definition Intermediates— the Significance of 24p. A white paper. Phillips Digital Video Systems, United Kingdom, 1998.

Bayes, Steve. The Avid Handbook. Boston: Focal Press, 2000.

Brenneis, Lisa. Final Cut Pro for Macintosh. Berkeley: Peachpit Press, 2000.

Dmytryk, Edward. On Film Editing: An Introduction to the Art of Film Construction. Boston: Focal Press, 1984.

Hollyn, Norman. The Film Editing Room Handbook. 3rd Edition. Los Angeles: Lone Eagle Publishing, 1999.

Kauffman, Sam. Avid Editing: A Guide for Beginning & Intermediate Users. Boston: Focal Press, 2000.

Murch, Walter with Coppola, Francis (Introduction). In the Blink of an Eye : A Perspective on Film Editing. Beverly Hills: Silman-James Press, 1995.

Ohanian, Thomas and Phillips, Michael. Digital Filmmaking. Boston: Focal Press, 2000.

Oldham, Gabriella. First Cut: Conversations with Film Editors. Berkeley: Univ. California Press, 1995.

Poynton, Charles. A Technical Introduction to Digital Video. New York: John Wiley, 1996.

Solomons, Tony. The Avid Digital Editing Room. Beverly Hills: Silman-James Press, 1999.

Webliography

NLE SYSTEMS

Avid

Avid's Official Website
http://www.avid.com
Avid's official site for product info and news.

Final Cut Pro

http://www.apple.com/finalcutpro
Apple's official home page for Final Cut Pro. The site features user tips,
downloads and information about upcoming releases.

Media 100

http://www.media100.com
Media 100's official site.

MATCHBACK SOFTWARE

FilmLogic

www.filmlogic.com
FilmLogic's official site offers downloads of trial version software, updates
and documents relating to use of FilmLogic and integration with NLEs, particularly Final Cut Pro.

Trakker Technologies

www.trakkertechnologies.com
Trakker's site offers trial downloads, documents and information about Sling-shot and Slingshot Pro.

NLE PERIPHERALS

Pinnacle

http://www.pinnaclesys.com
Pinnacle's official website. Information about Pinnacle capture cards and the latest HD cards available, including Targa Cine.

Aurora Video Systems

http://www.aurorasys.com
Aurora's 24 fps capture card, IgniterFilm, is featured here, along with a lot of other Mac capture cards that could be used for matchback.

USER GROUPS, FORUMS AND LISTSERVS

2-Pop

http://www.2-pop.com
2-Pop is an excellent forum for users of Final Cut Pro. There are message forums, product critiques, new ideas and an exchange of tips and methods for FCP users. This is not an official FCP site, but Apple has put some of its own FCP team members on the board to help users. Very popular place.

Worldwide Users Group

http://www.wwug.com
The ultimate forum for users of digital solutions. Covers Avid, Media 100, Final Cut Pro and much more. Each forum is hosted by an expert. There are also many informative articles posted here.

AvidEditor.com

http://www.avideditor.com
Great site for Avid users. Covers tips, job opportunities, discussion forums and more.

Avid Pro Net

http://www.avidpronet.com
User site for Avid users, hosted by Avid. Includes the Avid-L listserv, many articles by experts, some forums and a job hunter's area.

Ancient Avid

http://www.mag4media.com/avid.html
Promising new site for users of older Avid NLEs. Includes information about older NuVista Avids and their peripherals.

ADVANCED TECHNOLOGY

24p.com

www.24p.com
The 24p site is loaded with information about 24p technology, who's using it, where it's headed and so on. Articles, resources, links and more.

Phillips Film Imaging

www.phillipsfilmimaging.com
Look for updates on the latest developments with DataCine and other products.

Advanced Television Systems Committee

www.atsc.org
The Advanced Television Systems Committee (ATSC) is an international organization that is establishing voluntary technical standards for advanced television systems. ATSC Digital TV Standards include digital high definition television (HDTV) and standard definition television (SDTV).

International Telecommunications Union

www.itu.int
The International Telecommunications Union, headquartered in Geneva, Switzerland, is an international organization within which governments and private sector coordinate global television standards, including HDTV.

NEWSGROUPS

rec.video
rec.video.desktop
alt.movies.independent
rec.arts.movies.production

REFERENCE

Discreet

http://www.discreet.com
Discreet's website features information about their products as well as white papers containing a wealth of technical information about color space and HDTV technology

Keykode

http://www.kodak.com/US/en/motion/products/keykode/
Kodak's Keykode site, with diagrams, Keykode ID numbers, 35mm and 16mm test films, a post production manual and more.

Zero Cut

http://www.zerocut.com
Alan Stewart's excellent site features news and information regarding film formats and standards, 2:3 pulldown, HD developments, and DV transfer to film. A source of inspiration to this book, Alan's focus is primarily for Avid users, but the specs and workings of film with respect to NLEs are universal. Great articles and information.

The Motion Picture Editor's Guild

www.editorsguild.com
Information about the Editor's Guild, including rates, initiation and fees, and interesting articles. The Guild sets the standard for working editors everywhere. Even if you're not in the Guild, your pay rate is based on their work.

Filmmaker.com

Excellent site covers all aspects of filmmaking. Lists of resources, forums and up-to-date information.

SITES FOR EDITORS

Editor's Net

Post Industry. Com

http://www.postindustry.com
One of many sites geared toward editors.

Editor's Net

http://www.editorsnet.com
Much like Post Industry, but with a little more longevity.

Index